From Trauma to Sanity

Perseverance is Key

Valorita Salaam

 FriesenPress

One Printers Way
Altona, MB R0G0B0
Canada

www.friesenpress.com

Copyright © 2021 by Valorita Salaam
First Edition — 2021

The contents of this novel is based on my perspective of life experiences.

ISBN
978-1-03-911686-3 (Hardcover)
978-1-03-911685-6 (Paperback)
978-1-03-911687-0 (eBook)

1. FAMILY & RELATIONSHIPS, DYSFUNCTIONAL FAMILIES

Distributed to the trade by The Ingram Book Company

Table of Contents

Dedication

THIS BOOK IS DEDICATED to my husband whom I love dearly without measure and to my children who give me reason to be better. I also write this story in memory of my parents, who I believed loved me as best they could, and I accept this. And last, I dedicate my story to my friend who made herself available to me through all the struggles, good times and bad, thick and thin to the end; she knows her name.

Forward

THE BEAUTY OF FAMILY is closeness, love, trust, friendship, familiarity, and camaraderie. The other side of beauty can be pain and struggle; on the other side of pain for me is peace.

Names were changed to protect the privacy of individuals; this book is my perspective shaped by experiences.

I answered the phone with a whisper,

"Hello?"

"May I speak to Valorita Gill?"

"Speaking," in my whispered voice.

"Hello, did you say this was Valorita Gill?"

"Yes."

"Ma'am, why are you whispering?"

"So he can't hear me."

"So who can't hear you?" she asked.

"The man."

"What man?"

"The man on the roof."

"What man on the roof?"

"The man who sits on the roof outside my kitchen window."

"Why does this man sit on the roof outside your window?"

"I don't know; he just sits there watching me."

"How long has he been sitting there?"

"I don't know; maybe a few months."

"Well, ma'am, can I call you Val?"

"Yes, sure." I continued to whisper.

"Val, do you have another phone in the house?"

"Yes, there's one in the living room."

"Okay, Val, put the phone down and go in the living room and take the phone off the hook. Can you do that?"

"Yes, I think so, but I have to be quiet, so he doesn't hear me…"

INTRODUCTION

My DADDY TOLD ME that when you are little, everything seems normal if everybody is going through the same thing. My parents married when my mother was fifteen and daddy twenty-two; he said he thought she was older, and my mother said she pretended to be seventeen. I was the middle child of fourteen with three older brothers, four older sisters, and six younger sisters. In my family, we were all the same because happiness, hunger, sadness, and struggle was a shared experience. By the time I turned eight, mother and father had separated and later divorced. From then on I had "stepfathers."

As each man would leave our home, they left physical scars easily visible to the naked eye; however, it was the mental and emotional damage that was a mystery to my young psyche. I saw my mom struggle to raise her fourteen children alone, and as a young girl, I witnessed firsthand the dysfunctional dynamic of our family structure. With rarely a tear shed, Mother kept a strong face in public and around her little girls. Though she was sometimes a loving parent, at other times, she was cruel with her punishments of divisiveness and decisive separation between her children. To Mother's credit, she did her best to instill in her children the importance of religion, morality, and being respectable people of color. We learned to take pride in our heritage and stick together as a family. The other lessons were carefully woven into the fabric of our family from the oldest to the youngest child. The oldest children were taught to take care of younger ones, primarily because we were all born stairstep in ages and mother could not possibly care for her babies while expecting another child within the year. And while cruel to have young children taking care of even younger children and doing house chores, this is how the home was kept together. Mother would checkout of her responsibilities, as she was without a support system and overwhelmed by so many children. She was an only child, as was her mother and so on, but she wanted ten children—five girls and five boys—which she thought would make her happy. What Mother did not know was how much time and energy were required to take care of children alone.

My mother was physically beautiful and intelligent, despite not having a higher education. She could converse with scholars because her mother had taught her the intricacies of being a well-rounded woman. My mother had passed these teachings down to her daughters, yet somehow along the way, she had appeared to get lost in what she should have been doing while battling with what she wanted to do. These periods left me feeling abandoned and lost as if it was an inherited trait to carry until I could figure out my role as a young girl, woman, wife, and mother, and not necessarily in that order.

Some of my sweetest memories are from the time I spent with my seven sisters closest in age. We not only played together as children do, but we also got into mischief on the playground and around the house together. We were punished together and we cried quietly together, wishing one day we could live in a beautiful home with enough food to eat, clothes to wear, and toys to call our own. Since we were separated during the day while school was in session, as each of us were in different classes, meeting up afterward was welcoming and familiar. We played outside on weekends until the streetlights came on, coming into the house sweaty and dirty and being instructed to wash up for dinner. The older sisters took to the evening task of preparing the younger ones for bed, only to start the day over. Early on, I learned the importance of doing things right the first time, mainly to avoid being punished. This lesson would help shape my future, tainted with other hard lessons required for not yet realized survival.

We were all taught how to take care of the family—grocery shopping, paying bills, and stepping in for Mother when she was not present. I was the last child to carry the adult responsibility of raising the younger siblings; however, my turn had come too soon. In 1973, at the tender age of fourteen, I started taking on adult responsibilities. I became the shepherd of the house, which prevented me from experiencing life as a teenager. The dark days of hunger, brutality, loneliness, and abandonment hardened me for many years. Early on, coming from a large family taught me to fight for my life and challenge the anger brewing inside of me. Early battles on the playground taught me the importance of winning and filled me with audacity, for life got tough, and the struggles required inner strength. Each circumstance had a lesson attached to it, and every lesson built me up for the next event in my life. The twists and turns that followed after I left my mother's house required vigor, faith, backbone, and courage because my life became a nightmare.

My last psychologist told me I had experienced a tremendous amount of trauma, and I had learned how to push it down. He said it was a toxicity that needed to be flushed out for my survival. This is my story of survival from trauma to sanity.

THE EARLY YEARS

SOME MEMORIES PROVIDE THE time, weather, what was worn by whom, and so on. Others make me sad, smile with glee, or stop me in my tracks, frozen in time, trying to gather the whole scene with vivid clarity. Then, the memories are filed away for later, only to be forgotten as one day flows into the next. However, there are days when I pause to affirm the feeling. For instance, one day, while frying chicken, I heard a song on the radio, and a wave of sadness enveloped me.

I picked up the phone and called my best friend Serena. "My childhood was rough, wasn't it?"

She said, "Yes, my friend, it was." The phone call ended, and I went back to preparing my evening meal. I was saddened for a while, but after a short period, I snapped out of my reverie and came back to the present.

As a child, life at home had its ups and downs, and I had more than my share of work. It seemed like my days revolved around taking care of the house and my younger siblings. Serena reminds me of times past and how, as teenagers, we would talk on the phone nonstop about our weekend plans. She said I always had to cook and take care of the house while she planned outings with friends. She said she noticed how hard my life was, having to take on parental responsibilities, while her mother took care of her. I guess I do not know how that really feels—being taken care of by a loving parent.

One of my earliest memories is when we lived in the "Washington Park Homes" project high-rise on 44th and Cottage Grove in Chicago. I was being chased home by a group of boys who said they were going to beat me up because they liked me. I came home that day crying after the scuffle, and my mother told me the next time I let those boys beat me up, she would whoop my butt as well. The next day I let them chase me almost to my front door. I made sure Mother was watching, and I proceeded to fight each one individually. I was in the first grade, and my mother rewarded me with ice cream. From then on, I didn't have many more fights: word got around that I kicked butt.

Though quite young, I learned how to take care of my physical self and fight back against anyone trying to hurt me. Our family routines were the same as other families in the neighborhood. We did housework on Saturdays and went to church on Sundays and sometimes had a big meal afterwards. Kids could go out to play after twelve p.m., and when the streetlights came on, all the kids ran home. Playing outside with friends during the week was sparse because of school, while on weekends, the swings, monkey bars, sliding boards, jump rope, hopscotch, jacks, and silly games kept us entertained for hours at a time. Of all the fun we could imagine, nothing was better than bathing at night and being swathed in baby powder, with fresh hair, clean pajamas, and clean sheets. We hardly ever had any snacks, and sometimes, bedtime stories were heart-jerking, bittersweet memories. Sometimes our playtime was interrupted by a sudden eruption of gunshots, causing everyone to scatter from the benches and playgrounds to seek shelter. If you were in your apartment, the shots might bounce off the concrete walls outside of the building, forcing you to hit the floor until the shooting stopped.

Sadly, nothing, not even random gunshots during play, prepares you for your mother walking around with a black eye and a butcher's knife in her robe pocket; I suspected my mother was abused in her relationships. A saddened look on your mother's beautiful face while she struggles to survive is a pitiful memory for a child. That is just the way it was, our dark secrets were tucked away from public viewing. From the outside, we were well mannered, apparently happy-looking children, while on the inside, we were living with fear, anguish, hunger, and a battered mom.

Around 1968, my mother accepted the teachings of the Honorable Elijah Muhammad, and we became Muslims. Christmas was only a few short days away when Mother called us all in from our bedrooms and made the announcement. Afterwards, she instructed the older kids to take down the tree and told the little kids to pick one gift to keep: the others would be donated to kids who didn't have toys. I remember thinking, *Other kids without toys? We're the kids with hardly any toys.*

All the girls had to change from public to private school and stop wearing regular clothes like the other kids. We could not wear shorts, T-shirts, short dresses, or even swimsuits on the rare occasion we went to the beach. Instead, we wore long uniforms with headscarves to school and similar clothes at home. The school bus picked us up and dropped us off in the afternoons. We would rush upstairs in hopes of not being seen because we were teased and ridiculed for being different.

As early as I can remember, my dad never lived with us; he and Mom were long since separated by the time I was five or six. But I always saw him, whether he was in the neighborhood on the benches outside the basketball court or down 39th street where he lived. When I got a little bit older, there were times when no one was looking, and I would sneak away by cutting through the breezeway, going around the back of the building, across the parking lot of the next building, and walk down to see my daddy. It seemed like the longest walk, but it was always worth it. My daddy was pretty with his slick, shiny hair, cool cigarettes, and a beautiful smile. He wasn't tall—about 5'5"—but back then, he was a giant in my eyes. He was shining shoes whenever I visited. He would be busy either rubbing black polish on the shoes or slapping the shoes with a li'l spit to bring out that glossy shine.

Daddy would look up at me and say, "Red, yo' momma know you walked down here?"

Shyly, I would reply, "Naw daddy, I snuck away." He would humor me for a li'l bit, give me a quarter, then send me home. This routine went on for a little while until we moved out of the projects to the west side of Chicago. That was when life turned dark.

I was about eight years old when we moved and Mother disappeared. The older kids now had to take care of the younger ones. Life became miserable but being with my sisters eased some of the pain of missing my mother. This pain seems normal when you don't know any better. Being extra cold in winter, crowded in bed, and hardly ever feeling full after a meal is just a part of life. I learned to survive and live with what I had. I learned to respect and obey those who took care of me. So, when my oldest brother stated he would whoop my behind if he was awakened from his sleep on a Saturday morning, I learned to laugh quietly. When it was time for a whooping, I learned not to move my hand, or the count would start over. I tried my best not to flinch the slightest bit because even if the number of hits was at forty-eight or fifty and I flinched, the count started back at one. Another brother punished us by lining all the girls up in two rows with only a few inches in between. He would instruct one sister to walk between the rows and not touch anyone or else she would get a whooping. I learned not to move because if I swayed and caused the touching, I would be in trouble too.

It became normal to learn how to street fight at home. My brother Clay said, "It's my job and I'm gonna teach y'all how to fight because one day I'm not gonna be there to help you and you gotta know how to defend yourself." I started fighting my sister for practice. I would bloody her nose or blacken her eye and pull out her hair just to prove I could take care of myself in case I was ever caught alone. Normal to me was being pinned down on the bed on a Saturday morning with my favorite sister on my back and my hair wrapped in her hand. She was told how to pull my hair and hit me in the face with a balled fist. I learned to endure pain. This hard lesson was designed to save my life or my sister's life one day in the future. I endured the pain because she was smaller but older. I couldn't stop it and would not because this was the only way she would ever beat someone bigger than her. When the beating was all over, she was hailed as a hero, boxing champion style on the shoulders of the tallest, and touted like a winner. Battered and bruised, I was left to fend for myself.

While in the bathroom, through the tears and agony, I saw my bruised face. I squinted in the mirror at my new black eye, fat lip, pulled hair, red, blue, and green blotch marks on my light skin, and green dots in my left eye. I saw my pain in the mirror and cried. I was not mad at Coral; she won the unfair fight that was set up in her favor. Instead, I went to the store and bought some cocoa butter to help heal and prevent scars. I wore a brown printed scarf pulled down over my face to hide the bruises.

To my surprise, when I got home from the store, Mother had come to visit. I would be saved! She would deal with my abusers! But my excitement was short-lived. I was threatened: if I told Mother what happened, I would get it worse after she left. "You know she's going to leave," taunted my tormentors. So when Mother asked me what happened, I told her I fell down the stairs because the hallway was dark.

She said, "Be careful next time." After a short period, she left. Life in Mother's house was a challenge.

A hungry child does not only dream of food; the stomach is not the only empty place. For me, the hunger was for my mother's presence and my father's love. During these times, I found solace in playtime with my sisters. Playing filled the void food could not because food is temporary. Nevertheless, hunger pains and no mommy or daddy were accompanied by sadness and fear. The brutal fight, led on by my older siblings, had left me scarred on the outside and showed me how untrustworthy loved ones or people who say they "love you" can be and how they can hurt you deeply. Coupled with Mother telling me that I had to be more careful after the fight, then leaving me with my older siblings, I decided I needed to be stronger. I believe it was in that moment with my mother that I decided I would no longer be prey to anyone wishing me harm. My resolve gave me strength, and with that strength, I figured I would be okay.

After about a year, Mother moved all the girls to a spacious and beautiful apartment on North California Street. Our brothers did not move with us and to be honest I do not know where they lived during this time. Nonetheless, the happy times returned because Mother was once again living with us. By then, things were not terribly difficult as I became friends with other girls my age at school. Having friends at school was comforting because I now had an escape from home life. This time in my life was memorable, as I learned about God and how to behave like a young lady. Mother was adamant about displaying proper social behaviors, and her expectations for her daughters were high standards to meet. Our extracurricular activities at school were geared towards how to be good Muslim girls, and at home, Mother instructed us in etiquette behaviors.

In her best efforts, Mother taught us proper manners, good posture, and how to hold conversations. She also instilled in us the importance of learning about Mother Africa: she always told us we had a home in the eastern part of the world. These classes were rigorous and important as Mother imparted on us that young ladies were to be seen and not heard. It is sometimes difficult to understand why she was disappointed years later when we exhibited less than desirable habits. I figured she would relate our behaviors to her absence and lack of guidance, but that didn't seem to occur to her. The upcoming years became defining moments in my life as this new space with Mother presented other learning opportunities.

When my oldest sister Opal was around seventeen years old, I was amazed with watching her daily routines. I did little things to help her get dressed like ironing her clothes and picking tiny lint off of her knit sweaters—I guess my little nimble fingers made that a swift task, or maybe that was to teach me how to take care of my clothes. Either way, I felt special to be allowed in the room during this private time. I watched her as she burned the tip of an eyebrow pencil and lined the bottom and top of her eyes. She would then draw in her eyebrows and put on eye shadow and other makeup. The fabric of her soft stockings, underwear, and bras were amazing as mine were all a simple cotton. Stolen kisses, petting, touching, and wearing makeup and stockings were early learning stages—a rite of passage. My three older sisters Opal, Jade, and Saphire were an enigma to me, as they had their feminine ways with monthly cycles, hairdos, and sultry voices on the phone. They cooked our meals, combed our hair, and took care of us all while they were just teenagers. I never really saw their friends; I could only grasp what I saw and attempt to make sense of the abnormal.

Mother had a presence in the house but was never really there because she was again going back and forth between the two families. The rent was paid so we were never evicted or put out on the street, but the food . . . Where was the damn food? And the lights. Why did it go dark so often? And where was the heat? Why did the heat have to get turned off in the dead of winter? We put up thick drapes in the doorways to keep the heat from the stove in the central part of the house, where we spent most of our time. We were on welfare, and I did not know what that really meant, but I remembered always getting a check from the government. Yet, during these troubled times, I had my closest sisters in age with me always—Coral was a year older than me, and Diamond, the twins Pearl and Ruby, Amber, Jasmine, and Beryl were all younger. We shared food, clothes, laughter, teasing, tears, and growth together. We spent so much time together, and the love felt natural, real, and trustworthy. That pure love left me years later and never returned. I would spend my life trying to recapture that initial high of my first love with those girls. Mother had a way of controlling it all in her absence as I now accepted the new living conditions without her in the house—the bad and the (rarely) good; somehow, I survived another year.

Mother moved us once again, this time closer to where she had been living with her "other family." Mother had become involved with a man with nine children whose mother had recently died. This man made arrangements to move us out of the projects, but Mother had to stay with him to raise his motherless children. I suspect Mother thought it would be okay since she had trained her children to take care of themselves. She didn't realize the damage she was causing. Our brothers Clay and Lem came home too, but Terrel, the youngest brother, was gone; I think Terrel decided he could figure out his own life and help Mother more in his absence by not being a burden.

We transferred from private to public schools and I had to make new friends, but more importantly, Mother was around more frequently. While I never knew what kept her away from me, as I was one of the little kids not afforded the luxury of knowing grown folk's business, I was momentarily happy. When I was older, I learned that mother had told a close Muslim friend about her relationship with this new man and was reported for having relations without being married. In the Muslim community, this was a punishable act. Mother and her minor children were expunged from the Nation for one to five years. All this change caused me anxiety and damaged my young psyche. When I became old enough to piece my puzzled childhood together, the constant friction and change started to make sense regarding why she disappeared so frequently.

Shortly after moving to Schiller Street, I met my mother's Puerto Rican family. My siblings and I hated them on sight and it was clear they hated us. We hated them because they had our mother, and maybe they hated us because she was not their mother. I do not believe that our "stepfather" was a nice man since, at times, Mother cried a lot, had bruises, and sometimes disappeared. The disappearances were not unusual for us, but on the other hand, the new kids worried something had happened to her. One time, Mother was gone for several days, then she came home and stated she had gone to Florida for a vacation, and sadly, it was cold. I remember being pissed when she came back because I could not figure out why she needed a vacation. Moving closer to Mother did not change much, as she was now running between two households. Though she sometimes cooked for them and us, not much had changed in how the house was structured. The older kids still looked after the younger ones, and my sisters and I found ways to entertain ourselves.

All the kids in both families went to the same schools according to our ages. There were times when we somewhat played well together, but we mostly kept to our respective families. The parents did not seem to encourage us all to get along or to spend time together as a family. It was always 'them or us' situations, peppered with slight pushes and kicks along the way when we got together or passed on the street. My family was considered the "little kids," despite at least four of the other kids being in our same age group. It seemed like we were supposed to play well, but that never happened. Though we tried to be nice and made small attempts to be civil, our hearts were not in it, and the more we came to know them, the less we liked the kids our mother cared for instead of us.

Our hostility worsened after a couple of months when they decided to call us niggers. Though we had pent-up hostility, we had not stooped to the name-calling level. We had never encountered racial slurs personally, however, we knew being called niggers by the kids our mother took care of was wrong. A slow brew of anger started to boil, but as time inched along, we simmered and found a semblance of peace. Sometime later, in the sixth grade, my friends at school wanted to fight my "step-sister" and her friends on Friday. Fridays were the days set aside to fight after school as they presented an opportunity to settle disagreements boiling up during the week and hopefully squash them so everyone could start the next week off fresh. I was with my Black school friends on our side, and she was on her side with her Puerto Rican friends. Just before the fight, I crossed over and declared she was my sister and I would fight with her. She then stated that she did not need any help from a nigger. That word again! I looked sternly at her, and a few seconds later, I crossed back over, and we proceeded to kick their asses. I went straight after her, taunting and punching her with, "I got yo' nigger!" I wailed on her until I was exhausted.

By the time I walked home, she was hugged up to my mother. Mother scolded me for not standing up for her, and I plainly said, "Stand up for her?

Hell, I helped kick her ass because she called me a nigger!" Poor mother, she was confused about whose side to take. Hmm . . . Take her daughter's side, who was disrespected, or take the side of the poor, beaten, and battered 'other' daughter? Needless to say, I got my ass kicked for fighting my "sister."

Months later, their father and our mother left on a Saturday. All the kids were left alone to do anything we wished. While my family was playing in the backyard, the other kids started to yell *nigger, nigger, nigger* out the back window. We tried our best to ignore them, yet after a while, we got fed up, marched up the backstairs to their apartment, reached into the window from the back steps, then grabbed and punched as hard as we could. They broke loose and came out the back door to continue the fight. The hostility from both sides spread onto the back porch, down the stairs, up the gangway, and into the front yard. It was a vicious brawl! Their hatred towards us and our mother and our pent-up frustration towards them for taking our mother away energized us to fight it out. My sisters and I were trained fighters, and we unleashed hell on them. We left them whipped and defeated on the ground, then went into the house.

A little while later, their sister Milagros approached our sister Jade demanding an apology. Jade knew nothing of the fight but when she was told what and why it had happened, she did not offer up an apology. They started fighting after Milagros called Jade a *nigger-bitch with hoodlum younger sisters*. Milagros then slapped Jade and got slapped back; another brawl ensued. It was all downhill after that.

The adults came home, sides were taken, punishments were handed out, and over time, peace was restored. The damage had been done, as we were only victorious to ourselves. Mother continued her relations with the other family while I sat back and witnessed the deterioration of a family without a mother present. At ten years of age, I started to formulate an opinion. Although not clear at this time, ideas were developing. There was something seriously wrong with this family, and I knew it was not normal.

When I was around nine or ten years old, Mother told me to go and ask the "stepfather" for something. The event left me running home. I went to the house in the front and carelessly walked in, as this was normal behavior. He was lying across the bed in the small front bedroom. I walked to the door, and I delivered the question as instructed by Mother, then he responded.

I do not remember what the dialogue was at the time. What I do remember is what he said just before I left, "Don't you wanna kiss your Poppi on the cheek?"

I said, "Not really."

"Just a little kiss," He said.

I went over to the bed to kiss him on his right cheek, and he pulled me close to him and attempted to kiss me on the mouth; I quickly turned my head. His lips were wet and felt nasty on my cheek. I yanked away from him and ran to the hall. He got up from the bed and came after me as I opened the door. Fortunately, the kids who lived upstairs had just charged in through the front hall and ran up to their apartment. Their commotion stopped him in his tracks, and I ran out the front door. I ran down the stairs and around the back of the building as if my life depended on it. I ran to the cottage house, up the stairs to the second floor, opened the door, closed it, and locked it. Then, I ran to the bathroom, closed the door, and sat on the floor. Breathing hard, I wondered why a grown man would try to kiss a little girl. I thought it was unusual and strange but never told anyone. I came downstairs sometime later, and he was in the house doing something with Mother. He looked strange to me; it was then I vowed never to be alone with him again. The morning that spared me from being molested taught me a valuable lesson: Never trust "stepfathers!" As time went by, I never thought about the incident, and it would be a lifetime before sexual harassment caused me to question my decisions and impact my life.

*****

One day, Mother came in and said we were going on an outing of some kind. We excitedly dressed and headed out the door. We all marched down to the corner in a line of two-by-two, holding hands with Mother in the lead and the two older sisters in the back. We wondered where we were going until Mother stopped a police car and asked the officer to take us to the station. We waited for another car to arrive because all of us could not fit in one car. As scared little kids, we wondered what was happening. When we arrived at the station, all the kids were told to sit on benches in a holding room of sorts, and Mother left to talk to someone in charge. Other officers walked by and shook their heads, and then I heard someone whisper it would be sad to split us all up. Upon hearing this, my two older sisters Jade and Saphire left the room to find out what was going on. Unfortunately, my sisters were told that Mother wanted to put us all up for adoption since she could not do it anymore. My poor mother had a nervous breakdown and wanted us out of her life. My sisters asked to call our father, who later came to the station and took us home. Our mother was admitted into a facility for short-term care, and it would be six weeks before I saw her again. The man she had been living with was a monster, as I, too, had experienced.

I learned to be tough. I walked with my head up, shoulders back, stomach tight, like a football player walking up to the ref for the coin toss. I became quick with the tongue, biting words to talk down my opponents when they insulted me. A bully of sorts, always prepared to spar with anyone I thought was against me or my younger sisters. We called it the dozens and I was good at calling out those who did not like me and made them feel they had made a mistake when they chose to pick on me. I didn't know what the reason was for some girls and boys wanting to pick fights with me because initially all I wanted to do was make friends. However, my tall, skinny frame and knock knees became the subject of ridicule in the seventh grade.

There was a group of boys who teased me relentlessly in class, so in turn, I bullied the least attractive girl I could find. The more the boys teased me, the worse I treated the other girl. After school, the boys would chase me home and when they caught up with me, they would sting my knees by shooting pins off boomerang styled rubber bands. With bleeding knees, I would limp home crying to my mother. My knees would swell up only to have the same torture days later. As if the boys cared, they would space out their days of torture only for me to heal so they could do it again.

At the end of the school year, around 1970, we visited Opal, who had moved out and was living in the Altgeld Garden Homes on the far southside of Chicago near Riverdale. The visit lasted for the entire summer break. Our youngest brother Terrel came by one weekend and privately told Opal, Jade, and Saphire we would have to stay for the summer. He said the "stepfather" had burned the house down—both buildings—collected the insurance money and disappeared with his children. I did not know where my mother was.

By the time fall came around, me and nine of my sisters moved into an apartment with Clay and Lem. Our Grandmother lived across the hall. The building was a three-story walkup, with two units on each floor, in a mixed neighborhood of Puerto Ricans and Blacks on the north side of Chicago. This environment was very new to us as we had never lived too far away from people who looked mostly like us; we were now a minority amongst other minorities. Even the grocery stores smelled different as their ethnicity was unfamiliar.

On the street corners were many men and women who looked like me in complexion, but were culturally very different. The area was busy, and it seemed people stood around socializing more than being productive. Since obscenities were the only words I knew in Spanish, I recognized a lot of cursing in conversations. The men were plentiful and disrespectful when women and girls walked by. Seeing them pinch women's butts as they passed by or follow them down the street gave clear warnings of what would happen to little girls if they too came near them. As such, we crossed the streets in the middle or jetted between parked cars and anyplace else to avoid men and mischievous boys. We never went to the store alone in fear of being followed or touched by any of the men or teenage boys loitering on the corners.

Sadly, Mother was still not home with us, and living with Grandmother, who was mentally ill and very unstable, was scary. We never knew when grandmother would be sweet and loving or batshit crazy. She would either lovingly hug us, cuss us out or talk to her shadows. Sometimes, I could see the sweetness in her eyes, but as a child, I was afraid of her erratic behavior, never knowing what to expect. Again, this was all normal to me. But what wasn't normal was looking in the oven for pot roast and potatoes only to discover roaches in the gravy and then being scolded for not eating. Yet, I always had my sisters to play and make up games with. We always found ways to have fun, despite Grandmother's strange behavior. These were my sisters, my comrades, my first friends, and my family. We slept in the same bedroom, we bathed together, shared clothes, and watched out for one another. If you had a problem with one of us, you had a problem with all of us. Back then, I believed we were a package deal.

Around 1972, Mother moved us again, this time back to the southside of Chicago in South Shore near 71st street, and re-enrolled us in the Muslim school. There were ten girls and Mother in one apartment, and life was decent. We lived in a beautiful brownstone that had one apartment on each of the three floors. Our days included going to school and doing house chores. The oldest child was always in charge. We were raised in a hierarchy in which the eldest person always had the authority to boss the youngest ones, and you had to respect the leadership. During this time, Jade had a boyfriend, and like any other teenage girl, she stayed on the phone all day and forgot to do her weekly assigned chores. She was my bully, and it was tiresome. After some time, I got tired of being pushed and teased in the home. I got fed up and decided enough was enough and refused to take any more ass whoopings for things I did not do. On one such occasion, Jade decided to stay on the phone all day talking to her boyfriend. After several hours of being on the phone, she told me to clean the kitchen. "Nope," I told her. "It's not my turn to wash the dishes."

Washing dishes was labor-intensive in a house with eleven people. I decided I was not going to do her chores. Jade kept telling me to do it, and I refused. Eventually, she realized I would not do as told, so she proceeded to force me. We were about the same size by then, and I was just as strong, so when she attempted some force, I resisted with somewhat equal force. She pushed and dragged me up the hall to the kitchen. I grabbed door jams, stoppers, screamed, and yelled to no avail. She struggled, and I resisted for about forty-five minutes. In my loss, she forced me to stand up at the sink to wash dishes. I was sweating, exhausted, and defeated, yet determined to find a win. I decided to wash the dishes in cold water, then dry them to make them look clean. Then I waited for Mother to come home. Knowing Mother would request a glass of cold water, I made sure I was near. I was first to jump when she asked for that glass of water. First, I ran the glass under hot water to release the cold grease, carefully filled the glass with cold water, and put a napkin under the bottom to not drop the glass. As soon as mother gripped the greasy glass, it slipped from her hands and hit the floor, shattering glass everywhere. When asked who washed the dishes, Jade came from the back and said she did.

I got my revenge. No, this is not healthy, but this is me, a work in progress always trying to do better to offset my not so flattering ways. I loved my family and did what was necessary to keep us together, but as a teenager, I had an attitude. I did not realize where the emotion came from; however, I had to have payback whenever I recognized I had been treated unfairly. Somewhere in life, I had learned to be vengeful towards my loved ones, which was bad news for Terrel.

Terrel came back to live with us just as I became a teenager with audacity. One morning before school, Terrel was walking down the hall, and I noticed he was bowlegged. I teased him relentlessly, and to shut me up, he popped me in the eye. Not a good look, as my eye became swollen and turned a greenish-blue color. My mother told me I should not have been teasing him and sent me to school. I was angry and embarrassed, so when I saw a bigger girl pushing my little sister Pearl, I gave her a black eye. I was suspended from school for fighting.

Mother had zero tolerance for acting out in school and kicked my ass. I was pissed and rationalized I would not be in trouble if Terrel had not hit me. I needed to pay him back and thought long and hard about what to do. I devised a plan to use his bath time against him. Terrel enjoyed his nighttime baths. He would soak in hot water with Epsom salts after a long day of waiting tables. On this particular day, I asked Ruby if I could have her turn at preparing his bath. You see, mother had us practice pampering our brother so we could learn how to take care of our future husbands. She said that it was what good wives were supposed to do. We helped Terrel with his coat, massaged his shoulders and feet, and helped him with his slippers. We prepared his meals and ran his bathwater. This night he was in for a treat.

I ran hot water, a little hotter than usual, and instead of Epsom salts, I used table salt for his sore, blistered, cracked, aching feet. I stood outside the door and waited for the screeching sound of pain and laughed with delight. As soon as the door opened, I ran down the hall, maneuvered, slipped out of his grip, and ran back up the hall. While stopped at Mother's bedroom door, she came out to see her son soaking wet and butt naked in front of his little sister and was appalled. Nothing was worse than exposing yourself nude, and I made sure I pointed that out. But I was not done; the next day, I remedied the sleeping arrangements.

"Well, mother," I said. "He is a full-grown man, and I do not think he should be sharing a room with his sisters." I told her that I had found a room for him.

"Where?" She asked.

"The hall closet."

"That's ridiculous!"

"Not really. See?"

I showed Mother Terrel's new room. I had moved his twin bed and his nightstand into the large closet. I put all his suits, shirts, and ties on hangers above his bed and folded his clothes neatly on the shelves. It was tight as hell, but it worked. Besides, he needed his privacy as any young adult male, and his sisters also needed their privacy. Mother conceded, and I had the pleasure of escorting him to his new living quarters. I was the perfect hostess with the best manners when I kindly and lovingly proved to him how efficient his new living arrangements would suit him. He moved a few weeks later, and I like to think that I helped him become a responsible adult. He later married a beautiful woman, had five children, and recently celebrated more than forty years of marriage.

RESPONSIBILITY

THOUGH I STILL STRUGGLED with loving my mother, it did not interfere with the close relationship I had with my sisters, which was invaluable. However, having a girlfriend outside of the family was completely different. When I was eight, I had made my first close friend when her family moved next door to us in the projects. Vivian also had a large family and a single mom. We clicked instantly, and I was happy to have a friend outside of the family. When we moved from the projects, her mother let her visit. I met my other friend Serena in the fourth grade at the Muslim school. She already had a group of friends, and they welcomed me into their circle. Mother had taken us out of public school and put us in the private Muslim school when I was in the fourth grade, then transferred us to public school before the year completed. I skipped the fifth and went to the sixth grade, and then mother re-registered us into the Muslim school; the adjustments were a roller coaster. By then, I had survived the trauma of living with the "other family I hated" and was now ready to venture out and find my place. Somehow, I managed to learn enough to skip the seventh grade and was now in the eighth grade. The girl I had met was still there with her friends. I silently observed them be a clique; they sat together, walked together, and exchanged notes and secrets. I wanted in. However, I did not know how to make it happen, so I just waited.

A few months later, after temple Sunday, Serena walked up to me and said, "You're Val, right?"

I said, "Yes."

"We're gonna be good friends," She said.

Dumbly, I said, "Okay." And just like that, I was in. I had friends outside of my family. Two close friends, Serena at school every day, and Vivian, often out of reach but never forgotten. Having two girlfriends made me feel more confident, and as I found an identity, I felt normal. Though I hung out with the crew, I bonded more with Serena, and I felt she was more of my best friend. We talked on the phone nonstop while we were away from school, and she and I became closer. As we grew through our teen years, we held each other's secrets. Completely different backgrounds and opposite family structures did not deter our friendship. Her parents were married with just four kids, and they lived in the far south suburbs of Chicago. She had experiences I could only dream of, and I shared nightmares she could never imagine. Though she was not rich, her parents afforded her what I thought were luxuries unimaginable. Luxury to me then was your own bed, a loving home, a mom who cooked, loved, supported you, and a father in the home who provided. As we grew older, we remained friends. Though we made different choices in life, she was my best friend to the end. She valued me as an individual, and I never felt beneath her. Her family's success gave me life! This was my initial exposure to the finer things, and I used her life as an example to be successful, but my success was many years in the making.

Around the same time of meeting my new bestie, I met Lance. We used modern technology for our first coincidental meeting—the rotary phone. One of my sisters had me call the Shabazz Restaurant to get her then-boyfriend on the phone. When I was told he was not there, Lance came to the phone to cover for this guy because they were friends. He knew my sister and assumed I was her and started talking. Once he realized I was the sister, his flirt game kicked in. Initially, I was unimpressed, but the smooth talker persisted and persuaded me to calm down my attitude, and we talked for about an hour. And that is how I met my first boyfriend.

We talked every day at around nine p.m., but we had never met. After several weeks, he said he thought he saw me after Temple. I vaguely remembered him, and he went on to tell me he initially saw me several months back when I was walking to school with my sisters on a cold January day. He had two definite memories of me and wanted more. At thirteen years young, meeting him face-to-face seemed impossible. My mother ruled with a heavy hand, and my teachings admonished talking with the opposite sex. Having a boyfriend was unheard of. Unless you were getting married, there was no reason to converse with young men. Some weeks later, I found out he was eighteen! Having never physically met him, I panicked, but I was already hypnotized! I knew this was wrong, so I learned to sneak around. I knew full damn well that my mother would kick my ass, but it did not matter. I fell in love without ever laying eyes on him. Mother eventually found out about us talking, and she handled it well. Maybe it was the look on my face when she asked querying questions or the stern consternation of my behavior. I think she knew I would take the ass whooping and any other punishment to keep him. However, she laid down the strictest rules possible, and I consented willingly.

After about three months, I snuck Lance over to the basement laundry room of the building we lived in and we shared our first meeting with a passionate kiss while I was sitting on the washing machine during the spin cycle. I was swept. Thankfully, the landlord came in; my virginity was still intact.

While it is never easy being raised by a single parent, being poor and having a large family makes it harder for everyone. My mom struggled to make it happen. Each year brought new challenges for everyone, and with the younger kids coming of age, the older kids gained some sense of freedom. But for me, my coming of age meant I oversaw the house by making sure we were all up and dressed for school and meals were served. I also had the duty of looking after my little sisters at school and on the bus home, standing up for them in the streets, and relaying matters of importance to Mother. This was what each older child had done for years, and in 1973 at the age of fourteen, it was my turn since Terrel, Jade, and Saphire each got married just months before we moved to the big house in the suburbs.

Mother married the nicest man in the late fall of 1973. One morning, instead of going to school, we went to the courthouse to witness the legal marriage to our only true stepfather. He was tall, thin, intelligent, and polite. He was a Muslim man who did not curse, smoke, or drink. He was not necessarily handsome like the Puerto Rican, but more importantly, he was a gentleman. Our mother married a man who treated us all with respect and was good to us. He provided for us in a way that to me was different, as he was kind when he spoke. He worked full-time as an editor at Muhammad

Speaks Newspaper, and he was also a musician. He played the piano, wrote music, and taught me the basics of piano playing. He had proved to be better than the other men who would sometimes occupy our home as a "stepfather." He moved us to the calm, relaxed suburban life in Stewart Ridge, and for a moment, he provided normalcy and safety during my teen years. A stark difference from my younger years— this was the first and only house we lived in. Mother worked and came home in the evenings. She was home every day, and I no longer wondered about her whereabouts.

I remember being especially proud of her when she had become an executive secretary and had her first business trip. I smiled as she prepared for her trip with a beauty shop treatment since she had not gone to a salon since I was younger. Life moved smoothly while living in a house with two parents and my sisters. Being that we were girls, mother limited our playtime outside, and when she worked, we were forbidden to leave the house. Lance still occupied whatever free time I could find. He visited sometimes during the week and on Sundays after temple. We still talked on the phone in the evenings. By the time I turned fifteen, we had learned to sneak around the house to be alone because primarily, our visits were supervised. As we got older, I became emboldened, flippant at the mouth and started resisting the rules. With raging hormones, we got ever so close to sealing the deal but stopped. All the passion we shared was put on ice when he came over one day and told me he had been cheating with a woman his age. As a result, we parted ways. Remarkably, I was not mad because I realized he was a man with needs, and I was by no means putting out. He called me regularly and slowly eased the communication when he saw I was okay. We parted ways before I turned sixteen and while he was still twenty. I was still a child and he was a man with needs. We lived our lives separately for a long while.

Though I had ended my relationship with Lance and I suffered a broken heart, nothing had changed between me and my sisters. I became an avid reader and concentrated on making excellent grades in school. My sisters and I grew closer as we learned to depend on one another for activities and companionship. Our home was beautiful, we tended to our chores, and did our absolute best to make Mother proud of us, so when she came home she did not fuss. I made sure the house stayed clean, and the meals were served on time, and we cleaned up well after ourselves. We were well behaved and cherished the new life Mother and our stepfather provided for us. I learned the values of having a large family and many sisters as friends. Mother, however, never failed me in making stark realities hurtful memories on my soul, which later served as a point of reference for my endurance of pain.

Even though I took care of my younger sisters and had to report bad behavior, we had fun growing up and always found things to do for entertainment. We helped each other out with chores, played together, went roller skating, and had forced quiet time instilled by Mother. We also complained and confided in one another on sticky matters. When things were not going well around the house, we somehow managed to make it work. We played jokes on each other, cried together when we were hurt or sad, and mostly learned to depend on one another. When invited to parties, at least three of us showed up, and we always had dance routines to many songs. People assumed I was the leader since I was the tallest, but for Coral, who was a year older, that was not good because she was almost a foot shorter, so those younger than her did not take her commanding words seriously. What Coral lacked in height, she made up for in brawn, as she was tough. She was also very loving but somewhat uneasy since she had experienced life differently than me. She and I were extremely close because we had similar struggles as light-skinned girls in the hood. While I did not run into many conflicts, maybe because of my height, her stature and her mouth invited trouble. No doubt her gift of gab caused me to back her up numerous times because she would talk herself into fights that, realistically, she could not possibly win. I likened her to the Tasmanian devil from the cartoons. She would go into a playful situation, start some mess, and come out with dirt all over her and her hair pulled loose.

Another year had passed and, in 1976, we changed schools again. This time, I was separated from my youngest sisters when they were transferred to public middle school. Pearl and Ruby, the twins, were in the sixth grade when I got a phone call from the Principal's office stating they had to be picked up because there was a threat of an afterschool fight. I gathered the sisters at home, grabbed a bat and plenty of attitude, and walked the few blocks to the school. When we got to the school, there were crowds of people standing around anticipating a fight. We walked up to the door so that Pearl and Ruby could be let out, only to learn the twins were being held since they were the instigators. They had somehow angered the boys' football team, and some of the players wanted to fight two girls. "Outrageous" I thought as I gathered my sisters, then we proceeded to walk home.

While doing a headcount to make sure we were all together, I noticed the oldest, loudest, and shortest was not present. As we continued our walk home looking around for Coral, there was a commotion on the railroad tracks. Sure enough, there she was, running off at the mouth, stating how she could "float like a butterfly, sting like a bee" because she could fight like Muhammad Ali, all the while shuffling her feet, creating a white dust cloud from the rocks. *Oh shit*, I thought. *Here we go!*

In my attempt to guide Coral home, one of the football players grabbed my shoulders, so I questioned him, "Excuse me, you want that hand?"

He said, "What'cha gonna do about it?"

I then balled my fist and hit him in the face. My sisters saw what I did, and the next thing you know, there was an outright brawl moving down the street. We beat their asses and made sure they knew not to ever come our way again with nonsense; then we went home. As we laughed and joked on the way home, we vowed not to tell Mother because she admonished street fighting, and we were young ladies who were supposed to be seen and not heard. She attempted to instill in us that cleanliness is next to godliness and other such mantras. This was Mother's way of raising polite and respectful young ladies. However, there were times when we had to defend ourselves, and our brothers had made sure we could.

Hours later, the police rang our doorbell and told my mother a complaint had been filed against her sons for beating up some boys at school. My mother stated she only had girls living in the home, so she was told to prove it. We were called to the front hall, and when the mother of the young boys realized her boys were beaten up by girls, she was embarrassed and pissed. She yelled something like, "Y'all got yo' asses beat by some damn girls?" Disgusted, she dropped the charges. We laughed, and our mother was ashamed to have been contacted by the police because of our behavior. In Mother's opinion, we should have maintained ladylike dignity and walked home. In my opinion, we had to fight for street cred. Such is life—moving, struggling, going to school, and trying to find your place. I heard that when you come from a large family, often attention is scarce, and you learn to get in where you fit in.

A person learns to do things to stand out. I think my way of standing out was to become the protector of my younger sisters, standing up to their bullies.

Although Mother pushed me into adult responsibilities at an early age, she also made sure I was her constant servant out of fear, loyalty, and respect. One day, Mother called us to her bedroom and asked me to sit on the bed next to her. Believing this to be a privilege, I obliged her with glee; however, it was time for a lesson. As Mother started chastising us for a simple matter, she felt it best to smack me on the back of my hand with a pink brush. I must admit, it did hurt, but stubbornness would not allow me to yield to the pain, so mother smacked me again. Stubbornly, I refused to say "ouch" and another smack came, then another.

Mother said to me, "Oh, you're not gonna say ouch?" Relentlessly, she persisted in smacking my hand until it was bright red, and the pain was immense.

I yelled, "Okay, damn it, it hurts; stop hitting me!"

Instead of being further chastised for cursing, mother said, "Okay."

The pain on the back of my hand was so bone-chilling that it started to swell. I went across the hall to the bathroom and attempted to soothe my sore hand under hot water. Feeling no relief, I went to my mother and showed her my swollen hand. Mother wrapped it in a towel, called a cab, and took me to the hospital emergency. After the doctor examined my hand and told Mother an x-ray was needed, he left, giving my mother time to warn me that if I told him how my hand was injured, she would kick my ass when I got home. Fearing Mother more than a stranger, I made up a lie when asked. We went home, me with a fractured hand and our family seemingly intact. The love, respect, and fear I had for my mother battled in my soul.

*****

After attending a private school where my classmates were all girls, entering public school in the eleventh grade proved challenging. The year was 1976, and Sister Clara Muhammad's School had closed its doors. All students had to find other schools to attend, and for my mother, she had her hands full with enrolling my younger sisters in middle school. Even though I still had the responsibility of watching over my little sisters in public school and keeping them out of trouble, I unfortunately had to figure out how to continue my education without parental guidance. I, along with Coral and Diamond, had to enroll ourselves in high school because Mother could not be bothered. It was an individual effort we each had, as Mother took little interest in making sure we completed this onerous adult task. The school was located on the southside of Chicago and was intimidating at first sight. It was gargantuan in size compared to my previous place of learning, and not knowing what to expect was frightening.

The differences from then on became more than a challenge for me. Coral could not adjust to the change and dropped out of school. Diamond and I on the other hand, walked into the front office and checked into Corliss High School. The task was not difficult as we each were given the paperwork for our mother to sign for our admittance. When that was done, we walked around the school to get familiar with the layout. We marveled at the design of the school. The gym was in its own wing while the classrooms were on several floors at the opposite end of the building. I went from changing between three classrooms to having a course catalog with dates, room numbers, and times.

By then, Mother had divorced our nice stepfather, and we moved back to the city to the Woodlawn area. I rode two buses to school each day, starting at around six-fifteen a.m., to attend the first class that started at around eight a.m. Our new home was in a depressed area on the southside of Chicago with a mixture of homeownership and Section 8 housing, until you reached 60th Street, where the University of Chicago was located. The University separated the lower income of Woodlawn from the educated upper-income residents of Hyde Park. Getting back and forth to school and learning to read a course catalog was a newfound challenge. My prior school was one level, one hall, with no confusion. The new school scheduled classes all over the building from one end to the other. Over the next few weeks, I got lost, was often tardy, and was mostly confused by the time I entered the class. The scheduling, time, and location of my courses were unclear. On one occasion, I attended a history class with freshman students and was laughed out of the classroom. I went from making excellent grades to feeling dumb and inadequate for not being able to read a class schedule.

Going to school with boys, too, was complicated. Not wearing a uniform caused me to be anxious because I had not kept up with fashion trends. Having to shop for school clothes was a difficult task. Being that I was tall, the pants were often too short in length. Dealing with acne and inept with makeup made me feel unattractive and deepened my insecurity as a teenager. The stress of not knowing anyone and being frightened of starting over worried me. My older sisters had married and moved on with their personal lives, which left me without guidance. Feeling inadequate in high school had become too much to endure, so I started skipping classes. When I returned after my first absence, I wrote the excuse and signed my mother's name. After a period of absenteeism, a classmate asked me what my mother thought about me missing school. I said she did not care. My absences went from one day at a time to three days, to a week. After I received my second-semester grades, which were all *F*s, I dropped out of school. I thought I would get a job and be productive with my time. Instead, I was confronted with a lack of jobs. Companies either weren't hiring or had a waiting list. It was a long summer that gave me too much time to waste and made me grow up fast. That was when I lost my virginity.

*****

In the summer of 1977, I started having unprotected sex. During that time, my girlfriends, sisters, and I did not have conversations about birth control as commonly as people do today, and getting contraceptives was no easy task either. I had gone to a private school during middle school and for two years of high school, where sex education was pretty much non-existent, and Mother had just moved back to the city from a Chicago suburb.

That old saying "blind leading the blind," well, that was Serena and me. We kept saying, "My period is late, but it will come tomorrow." After that it was "Oh, I see some blood; my period is here," but it was only a bit of spotting. Then it was, "it will come next week." This went on until I realized my period wasn't coming. We suspected I was pregnant, so I went to a Planned Parenthood clinic where Vivian's mother worked and took a pregnancy test.

At the age of seventeen, I found out I was pregnant. I was more than a few weeks along by that point. A counselor and I discussed my options: birth, adoption, or abortion. I went home and ignored the diagnosis and kept hanging out in the summer as if I were normal. I did not tell my girlfriends or anyone else.

We were poor, and my mom was on welfare. I knew how it felt to be hungry, cold, and to live without. Coming from a large family and struggling to make ends meet was an everyday experience. While I did not know what or who I would be in my adult years, I knew that I had zero capacity for being a young, unwed mother. Any child of mine would have to have a better life than mine. One day while in the bathroom, my lower abdomen felt hard, and I suddenly remembered that I was told I was pregnant. I feared what my mother would do when she found out! I was ashamed of myself and realized that I had to alter the situation somehow. I went back to the clinic and asked where to get an abortion. They said that I had run out of time for a regular abortion. My only other option was a second trimester abortion, which included a hospital stay. They gave me a list of references, and the rest was up to me.

I found Kaplan Women and Children's Hospital, a facility near my home, and I made an appointment. After my examination, I scheduled the termination procedure. The doctor's office called me back after a few days and told me that I had contracted an STD that had to be cured in order to have the procedure. Another humiliating blow to my psyche. Another clinic to find for people with low income to get free services. I received the antibiotic injection and shamefully went home. I told both of my girlfriends what had been going on, and they were both shocked. We were still wet behind the ears and did not know much about relationships, sex, or pregnancies. Outside of occasional babysitting, we had little interaction with girls our age who had been pregnant. I was the first one to screw up my life at seventeen.

I planned for the procedure, took my mother's Medicaid card, and told her that I was spending the night at Vivian's house. I checked myself into the hospital alone. The room was cold, and I was lonely. I was afraid but put on a brave face. It all seemed surreal as I signed a medical document that stated that in the event the fetus was aborted alive, though quite possibly deformed, I would take responsibility for the child. My procedure induced labor lasted for eight hours, followed by vaginal delivery. I cried and prayed for a dead fetus. How could I take care of a deformed child when I was attempting termination of what would, in all likelihood, have been a healthy child?

Later that night, after experiencing eight hours of painful labor, I gave birth to a dead baby boy. They put him in a shiny metal container with a lid. I was torn with emotion, exhausted, and afraid of what would happen next. I cried myself to sleep. The next day I checked out of the hospital and went back to my friend's house. I had cramps, bleeding, and engorged breasts. On the third day, I went home to check in with my mother, and my breast started leaking on the way there. Embarrassed, I covered it up and walked quickly up the stairs to change my clothes before seeing my mother. My body was going through the natural process after having delivered my first child. I learned then what it was to go into labor, give birth, experience death, and need rest. After a few days, my body healed, but I never told my mother about this trauma. My life experiences became more cumbersome from that day forward.

After healing from the abortion, I knew I was on the wrong track, so I became determined to complete high school. I went to the welfare office for guidance and was told about an alternative high school. In the fall of 1978, I attended the Loretto Adult Education Center on 64th and Dorchester since it was within walking distance from my home. I applied for General Assistance, a government-funded program that paid for alternative schooling and provided a small amount of money to those who qualified by being unmarried and without children. I enrolled, and it felt good. I made some new friends, became a cheerleader, and started having fun. However, it would be many years down the road before I addressed my childhood fears.

I managed to carry my armor for protection because I had serious trust issues. During this time, I lived at home with mother and seven younger sisters. I was in my fourth year of being in charge around the house and I was tired of not having a life. I never really experienced boys, dating, or hanging out with friends. Therefore, whenever a chance came to get out, I took it.

Socializing was awkward and trying to fit in was complicated. Still quite naïve in social surroundings, I started hanging out with friends at my new school. Students had to be eighteen years of age to enroll and some of my classmates were fifty years and older. One evening an older student invited me and my new friends over to her building. There was a rec room for our enjoyment. She supplied us with liquor and food then left. This was my first experience in a social setting of this kind and I was nervous.

I had my first drink of vodka, straight up, no chaser, and room temperature. It tasted awful and burned like hell on the way down as I drank it fast. The liquor hit my virgin system and I was lit. Not realizing what was happening, I got drunk quickly. I stumbled to the pretty pink bathroom and vomited all over the floor, wall, and finally the toilet. Sometime later, I was hoisted up, cleaned off, put in my coat, and taken home by my new friends. I remember stumbling, falling, and being dragged and pulled, all while being held up under each arm all the way home. Unfortunately, this would not be my only instance of drinking myself to embarrassment.

I now realize I was trying to fill the empty void of acceptance after being rejected by my mother as a little girl. In my mind, she preferred to love other children because I was flawed. I became insecure, angry, and defensive. I told jokes to mask my pain. If someone told me they liked something I had on, I would give it to them; I gave away personal items in hopes of making someone love and accept me for me. No one man or friend squelched my need for acceptance. I lived a life of longing and acceptance for many years. And while it would take many years before I obtained a semblance of peace, in the meantime I drank, laughed, and made people believe I was okay. No one knew the depths of my pain . . . I was a chameleon blending in with the family circles of friends, acquaintances, and society in emotional turmoil and pain.

As I drank, I became cynical and demanding. I had an inward smirk as I aged and started to think my destiny was etched in stone. I also became critical of other people's lives and judgmental about their choices. At the time, I didn't own my bitchy behavior nor did I concern myself with why people were moving further away from me. I believed it was their loss not to befriend me. I was fortunate to have life-long friendships, so it couldn't have been me, it had to be all these other people with the problem! Loneliness beseeched me and a lack of acceptance wreaked havoc in my heart. When you're cold, you find warmth, when you are hungry, you eat. So I drank to fill myself up, make myself warm inside, and mask my hunger.

How do you mend a broken heart when the heart breakers are your parents? Being rejected by my parents, unbeknownst me at the time, was unbearable. Unable to correct my destructive behavior, I built more walls. I had a chip on my shoulder as inward turmoil was sequestered out of fear of being seen as weak. In my second semester of school, I met my future daughter's father.

Decision Making

When I was eighteen, I moved in with daddy. Diamond, Pearl, Ruby, and I thought life would be cool since daddy was not as strict as Mother. How my sisters came to live with daddy was an interesting tale. While Diamond, who had just graduated high school with honors and a baby bump, and I just wanted to live with Daddy, however, Pearl and Ruby moved in by way of the custody courts.

At the young age of sixteen, the battling duo, who thought it was a bright idea to be known as the bad ass twin girls from the southside of Chicago, caused much trouble for Mother. In the mid-70s, it was still cool to street fight. What the twins lacked in height, they wanted to make up in brawn. It did not matter how dumb the goal was; to them, a reputation as a badass was an achievement. After being kicked out of two high schools—Roberto Clemente High School on the North Side and Hyde Park Academy on the southside—and after numerous fights, mother went to court. She told the judge she had done the best she could, and if she took them home, she would no longer be responsible for their care. At least that's what she told us after they had been missing for two weeks and we cornered her for an answer as to where they had disappeared.

Daddy, thinking her position was cruel, responded to the judge, with "Let me have my daughters. I will love and care for them far better than you ever could." Daddy later discovered their warped sense of judgment and delinquent behavior caused my mother to physically jump on them and eventually request their removal from her home.

The way the girls were in Mother's home was the same at daddy's house. They did not clean up after themselves or cook any meals. Worse was the lack of care each of them displayed about other people's property and the complete disregard for house rules, which baffled our father. Oppositely, they made sure they were dressed well for socializing and always had some place to go and boyfriends. When I visited, I noticed how daddy would come home and get pissed because neither of the three girls would make their beds, clean the house, or cook dinner. In fairness, they were accustomed to being told what to do, and they rarely cleaned up on their own since it had been my job to remind or tell them to do their chores. Also, it was either Mother, on rare occasions, or I who cooked their meals. They were lazy around the house, and Mother did not seem to expect much of them. They were low in the pecking order of household chores. For these reasons, I saw a way to move in, and I used their inabilities to my advantage. Daddy said that I could come because I would bring order. I took charge and made sure we went to school and met back up at home in the evenings. I cooked dinner and hung out a little with my friends and boyfriend.

At Daddy's, I began socializing and staying out after ten p.m. Shortly after I moved in, daddy took a vacation to Arkansas to visit with his parents and siblings. We were hurt because he did not ask or invite any of us to go to meet our grandparents, aunts, uncles, or cousins. I took this "opportunity" to ask my sisters if they minded if my boyfriend could spend the night while daddy was on vacation. They did not see a problem with it, and so it happened. I had my first adult sleepover. William came over, and as nighttime came, both of us were nervous. He started doing push-ups, I think to impress me, as I tried to be cute and watched, wondering what to do next. Needless to say, after wearing out the sofa sleeper, we settled down for the night. As if being told not to do it again, we woke up the next morning with some type of bites all over us. It turns out the sleeper sofa was infested with bedbugs and had to be thrown away. I never disrespected my daddy's house again.

As time went by, I asked my dad if it was okay if I spent the night with William. I justified my weekend getaway by telling him that all my chores were done, and dinner for the next two days was in the fridge. He looked at me over his reading glasses as if to wonder if I had lost my rabid ass mind! I then stooped down, kissed him on the cheek, sat on his lap, and said, "Daddy, please, I'm a big girl, and I'll be careful," and it worked. He said okay, and I left.

However, I was somewhat surprised because, once at William's house, he snuck me through the back door, and we crept up the stairs. I was taken aback because he presented the weekend as if his mother had approved. I went along since I was there, and though uneasy, I agreed to stay at his mother's house without her permission. I also looked past the disrespect of sneaking into the house for a chance to hang out with him for a few days. I crept around upstairs for the entire weekend, going in and out to the movies or restaurants. In the morning, he would go downstairs and cook me breakfast and sometimes take a long time coming back. He said that his mother would come into the kitchen and start talking. I did not get mad; instead, I enjoyed whatever he cooked. I was young and in love without the means to afford my own life. While still completing high school and making excellent grades, having a boyfriend during that time of my life was exciting. I had some new girlfriends, and I was relaxed. He and I hung out, went to the movies, and I started tasting wine. I was typical in some regards. I still had some house rules and a part-time job. The boyfriend fit well in my life.

After a few weeks, he took me to meet his grandmother. I was impressed with his close connected family. Most extraordinary was meeting his grandmother's sisters and their children. I did not have family ties beyond my parents and siblings. Meeting extended family members was new to me, as I knew very few of my father's siblings and their children, and my mother was an only child. As the girlfriend, I attended his family gatherings and celebrations. Unlike my family, where celebrations were scarce, his family seemed to find reasons to celebrate. They came together for graduations, proms, holidays, birthdays, and yes, funerals, of which I had little familiarity. After two years of fun, as it is in young relationships, ours turned sour. After all, it was a high school romance not meant to last forever. He was a pretty boy and a cheater. His family outings became infrequent occurrences, and our togetherness decreased. It was time to move on but breaking up was hard to do.

I concentrated on school, and in June, at nineteen years of age, I graduated with honors. I did not go to prom because William refused to escort me, and I could not find a date. For graduation, Diamond, Pearl, Ruby and Serena witnessed me walk across the stage. My dad said he could not get time away from work, and I do not remember where my mother was. I did not have a celebration party, gifts, or anything, but dear God, I graduated from high school! I afforded myself a small amount of joy for this important accomplishment.

*****

While talking on the phone with Serena one day, she mentioned going to school to be a court reporter. Very interesting! My mother was once an executive secretary, and I thought court reporting was a step up. I had another friend in the military, and he was a naval secretary. I was intrigued. I did not think college was an option because I didn't have any money. I thought maybe that was why I saw students taking tests in the library one day at school before the end of the semester. It had something to do with college and standardized testing, but since I did not ask anyone, I missed out on potentially going to college. I thought about enrolling in the police academy, being a model, or an airline stewardess. All these career options gave me ideas to get away from my sour relationship and do something positive with my life.

After serious consideration and not asking anyone for advice, I decided to join the military. I found a recruitment office and discussed my options. I got an appointment for the Armed Services Vocational Aptitude Battery (ASVAB) exam. I went to take the test, and to my joy, I scored enough points to join the Navy. My recruiter told me that I was about four pounds overweight at five foot eight inches and 151 pounds, so I was given water pills to drop the four pounds before my physical. I went down to the facility, and after a full day of evaluations and tons of paperwork, I was sworn into the armed forces naval branch. I promised to defend my country and be a steward for American justice around the world. I signed a contract, was given a leave date of April 17, 1980, and I felt competent and ready to move on in life. Exhilaration empowered me to share my good deeds with my parents! They seemed to be proud of me.

Weeks later, when I was sleeping at my mother's, I was awakened on a Saturday and told to clean up the house because we were going to have a baby shower for Diamond. She had become pregnant after graduating from high school. I was excited and proceeded to clean up. We did not have a vacuum, so I swept the carpet with a spray bottle of water until it met Mother's standards of cleanliness. Someone went to the store and bought snacks, and we decorated for the shower. My older sisters and brothers, with their spouses and children, arrived with gifts. Mother had bought a beautifully decorated full sheet cake for my sister with a baby carriage with blue and pink balloons.

I was surprised to see the cake had my name on it with a congratulations for joining the armed forces. The congratulatory addition seemed out of place on the cake, as if it was an afterthought. That did not seem right to me, but I did not mention it at that time. Joyfully, my little sister opened her gifts and was greeted each time with cute clothes, toys, and trinkets for her and the new baby. My mother bought my sister a beautiful slip with a matching bed jacket to be worn after delivery. I also received a gift from Mother: monogrammed stationery so I could write home in style. Coupled with my unhappiness at being an afterthought on the cake, this gift reinforced my hurt towards my mother.

"So, let me get this straight," I said to her. "I spend the entire day cleaning up the house for HER baby shower only to find out it's my party too, and all I get is a funky box of paper and envelopes?" I was pissed! I shouted, "Get pregnant fresh out of high school, and you get sexy lingerie and other gifts! Graduate with honors, join the military, and get some paper and envelopes! Well damn, didn't I earn some stamps too?"

The following weeks were a blur. I was counting the days before I was shipped off to Orlando, Florida, for basic training. The days ran together, indistinguishable, one from the next. I was having difficulty falling out of my high school romance and spent little time with family and friends.

I came home one night, and daddy said some guy called me. He had written down his name and number; it was Lance! I had not heard from him since I went to his wedding. Watching him walk down the aisle stung my heart a bit, but more importantly, I was happy for him . . . kind of. I remember feeling like I had lost my first love, and I was a little sad. These feelings resurfaced when I got the news he had called. I dialed the number, and it was wrong.

"Daddy," I yelled, "you wrote down the wrong number!" "Well, Red, he'll call back." Daddy shouted back like it was no big deal.

"He will call back? Really?"

I could not wait that long! So, I sat there and called every combination of those precious seven digits and was rewarded with his voice an hour later. Although I hadn't spoken to Lance in years, it felt like it was yesterday, and my heart relaxed. He said he saw my sister Coral, and she told him I was joining the Navy. He wanted to talk to me before I left. After about an hour of talking, we agreed to meet the next day. Though he said he was still married, I was single and did not care if it was right or wrong. Love and logic prevented me from staying away. He was my fire, and I wanted to get burned.

The next day, before he came over, I knew my white shorts were too short, and the belly shirt was inappropriate, but I wanted him to see me as a woman. I brazenly hugged him and sat across from him, legs crossed yoga style. We chatted, and then it got uncomfortable. We needed to get out of the house, so I asked him to drop me off somewhere, and we left. While driving down Lake Shore Drive, I realized I was in the car where his wife sat. I got eerily nauseated. Fortunately, his car started jerking, and he pulled off on the shoulder. His car stalled just a few blocks from daddy's house, and we parted ways. I started the journey home, which gave me ample time to ponder my unabashed behavior and feel the relief of his vehicle stalling. That would not be the last time we got together, and I somehow knew we were not done.

The rest of my time was spent alone, except for two occasions when I met up with my ex and got between the sheets. Then, out of the blue, I got a phone call from my recruiting officer, who said that a seat had become available and wanted to know if I was interested in leaving early.

"How early?" I asked.

"Well, next week." He said, "You could be in Florida on August 16."

Hey, that is the day before my 20th birthday. With excitement, I responded, "Yes!!!"

"Well, not so fast," he said.

"You have to go and get a physical."

"Oh, I'm healthy; I just had my annual two weeks ago."

"Well, we have to examine females before they leave to make sure they are not pregnant."

He sent a car for me and once back at the facility, I took a pregnancy test. I went home and thought that was that. I got another phone call shortly after, and the recruiter asked me why I left so soon.

"Oh, I was done, and they told me I could go home."

"Well, I'm sending a car to take you back; they were not finished with you."

In a confused state, I patiently waited for my ride while wondering why they told me to go home. When I got back to the office, someone mentioned that every day a girl is called back to the doctor's office.

I asked why, and someone said, "To tell her she's pregnant."

"Oh, I'm not pregnant; I just had my physical."

So yes, the doctor told me I was pregnant . . . again. I told him that it could not be true because I had just completed my annual; I was not pregnant and hadn't had sex since my annual physical. I guess I forgot about those two times with William.

The doctor advised me to get another examination because their equipment was "very sensitive," and sometimes it picks up things that are not there. They did not want to give me another examination at the free clinic because they, too, said I had just completed my annual checkup. After I told them my plans and said I needed their guarantee I was not pregnant, they gave me another test, which confirmed that I was indeed pregnant. Shock! Dismay! Sadness! Loneliness! Tears! What to do now?

After I told the recruiter I was pregnant, I had to sign various paperwork advising me of my options. I had two years after the signature date to rejoin. If I came back, I had to appoint a legal guardian for my child. *Wait; what? Abandoning my child was a viable option?*

Telling William was not easy because, in essence, we were no longer a couple. I had to endure the humiliation of being asked, "Is it mine?" His nerve! The cheater never was faithful.

"Yes, you are the father, and what do you want to do?" I responded.

He said, "I guess we can get married."

There was momentary elation as I told my parents I was pregnant and getting married. A few days later, William said he was not ready to marry me and since I was not in love with him, I had to make yet another hard decision.

After weighing my options and hearing that William's mother thought it was best we abort the pregnancy, we decided to each pay half for the abortion. A friend said she would loan me my portion if I could not come up with the money.

William and I briefly worked together at the Ringling Brothers and Barnum & Bailey Circus a few weeks after my pregnancy confirmation. While not a couple and I expected little from him, I wanted respect. The strangest thing happened one day at work. I had to go to the bathroom, and it was on the other side of the tiger cages. There were quite of few cages linked together, and as I was trying to figure out how to get around, I saw someone jump between two linked cages. In my haste to jump through the same two cages, a tiger lifted its tail and pissed in my face. I do not remember which was worse, the humiliation of being pissed on by a tiger or the burning in my eye! I rushed to the bathroom to flush my eye with cold water until I felt relief. I reached for the paper towels, and as I was patting my face dry, two girls were standing there staring at me. One of them said, "Are you William's girlfriend?"

"Well, not really," I responded.

"Are you pregnant by him too?" one of them asked.

"Yes, I am," I responded.

They turned their noses up and left. Though not realizing what had just happened, one thing was pretty sure, William got a girl pregnant who smelled like piss.

The night before the abortion appointment, William told me he did not have his half of the money, and he still did not want to be a father. I contemplated his words, and then it hit me.

"I'm not ready to be a mother either, but I cannot abort everything God puts in me."

"But I'm not ready, and you can't force me to be ready."

"That's okay. I am going to do this on my own. You will find me when you are ready."

"How will I find you?"

"Oh, you will; trust me," and I hung up the phone.

I felt relieved and resolved. I knew I had made the right decision. I was going to be a mother.

God's Gift of Love

My mother was always a religious person. She went from being a Catholic to a Black Muslim under Elijah Muhammad and then an Orthodox Muslim. As such, the private school I attended off and on was Sister Clara Muhammad's on 71st in Stony Island on the southside of Chicago. Under strict discipline, I was taught the importance of morality, virtue, spirituality, and marriage. Even though I fought vigorously with my mother, these principles formed me as a young girl and an adult woman. As I matured and learned my way, I still visited the mosque and attempted to govern my life with early learned principles and beliefs. However, once pregnant, I felt it hypocritical to attend without a husband. On the last day I attended, I wore a linen, peach-colored, calf-length dress that showed my baby bump. I did not feel clean or worthy, so I left.

*****

Accepting responsibility for my actions and deciding to parent a child alone is a mature decision. So is choosing to remain healthy during pregnancy. I took long walks and ate plenty of vegetables that my mother prepared. Though I lived with my father, I stayed in contact with my mother. I had so many questions and could not form the words to ask for answers, so instead, I spent as much time as possible with her. I visited the free clinic for all appointments until finally, someone realized the father and I needed to take a blood test. We had not seen or spoken to each other since our last phone conversation, and I was not forcing anything on him.

William was reluctant about going to the appointment but decided to go anyway. He met me at the clinic, and we took the test. After that, we went our separate ways until we were called in for another appointment. We were told we were not compatible to make a child. I asked what that meant. It meant since we both had the RH negative factor in our blood, I would more than likely give birth to a child susceptible to sicknesses. Another downer but not the worst, I thought. We did not speak again until the end of my second trimester.

Back at my father's, I continued to keep things in order before he came home from work. I lived with daddy to get away from Mother's strict household and to experience life. My decision cost me my freedom by getting pregnant, but little had changed between my dad and me.

As more time passed, hospital delivery was in question. The clinic assumed I was on welfare and had a medical card to cover the delivery. I was still on General Assistance, but the plan only covered me and not my unborn child. I had waited too long to sign up for a private hospital with an OB/GYN to care for me or deliver the baby. I was told I would have to go to Cook County Hospital and the thought of this terrified me because I suspected I would not be treated with kindness. Well damn! How the hell do adults do this? So many decisions and where in the hell are the answers? Are they written down somewhere? Is there a school of thought to learn from?

As I went home, feeling dejected and confused, I was happy to see my sister Jade. I told her my predicament, and remarkably, she was dating an OB/GYN! "Oh, I'll just call him and ask him what to do," she said.

Fortunately, Jade's doctor friend said that he would take me on as a patient even though I was six months along. He advised me to apply for welfare and medical. He started seeing me in his office and requested to meet the father. My ex was surprised to hear from me but agreed to come and take me to the doctor. After our first visit, he accompanied me to the remaining appointments and the birthing classes. To my surprise, my sisters gave me a baby shower and invited my ex's side of the family. I was happy to receive the gifts and some acceptance from his family for the upcoming birth of our child.

On April 27, 1980, I gave birth to a beautiful, cherub-faced, dark curly-haired little girl who weighed 7lbs 6oz. We named her Alicia. I loved every centimeter of her regardless of the horrific pain, which fractured her father's hand because I squeezed it so hard. Irrespective of the drugs they gave me to relieve the uncontrollable intense pain, I forgot the breathing techniques. I was overjoyed with her healthy birth even though I experienced the first and worse case of hemorrhoids. I was elated because I had given birth to a healthy child. I did not have to sign a contract taking responsibility if she was deformed. God blessed me with the wisdom to carry her to term. He blessed me to eat healthily, stay calm, take long walks, and not fight and argue or be mischievous and vengeful in my heart. I was so happy and blessed. Being a new mother felt good, and it was onward and upward. Everything would be okay, wouldn't it?

*****

A single mom and still living with my daddy, I found my first full-time job working in fast food. When Alicia was three months old, I started the five-day routine of leaving the house, taking my child to a babysitter, and going to work. I did not have a car, but public transportation made it possible to get around. I lived on 39th Street, the babysitter was on 69th, and I worked on 35th Street. I woke up early enough to get out of the house to start my day, and I was never late for work. Sticking to his word, the father was of little help during the week but somehow found time on some weekends to pretend to help by playing daddy. It seemed more like a show-and-tell episode that lasted longer than needed, but I did work on weekends, and in all honesty, this antic gave me at least one day of rest.

During the first year of being a single mom, I made sure to visit Alicia's great-grandmother. I realized the importance of teaching my daughter about both sides of the family regardless to how William and I viewed a parenting relationship; I wanted her to know her father's family, especially since I never knew my father's side of the family. Fortunately, they all seemed to welcome me without hostility and sometimes helped with the baby. William's brother and female cousin were especially helpful, and I appreciated their genuine love and support. I never asked anything about my ex, and I basically left him alone to figure out his life. I also did not set up child support, which in hindsight would have helped me out a lot. I did not want to force him to care since he said he did not want to be a father. I worked, paid my bills, and provided for my child without complaint.

Being that I never pressured him, and it did not seem he was interested in a family, I was somewhat surprised when he reached across the seat to hold my hand while driving somewhere in his mother's new car. I looked at him and asked what this was about, and he asked me if we could work things out. So, we started things up again when Alicia was not present.

After several months of working things out, I came home one Sunday and was surprised to find boxes all over the house. Confused, I asked my father what was going on. His girlfriend told me I had to move out. I again asked my dad what was going on, and he put his head down with a defeated look on his face and said, "Dorothy moved in." This trollop gleefully told me she had packed all my things and put them in plastic bags. As my eyes teared up, I gathered my stuff and left to move in with William at his parent's house because I had no place else to go. We lived upstairs in the area I used to spend the weekends while in high school. I was now living with William's family with a child and was still nobody's wife. And worse, William was still a cheater.

*****

Living with William and his parents proved challenging. My first Monday morning was business as usual, with zero support from him. My new address somewhat worked as I now started down the street from the 7800 block to the babysitter and then to work. Working hard and making little money, I was financially below the poverty line and qualified to receive welfare for my daughter. I paid my bills, which included rent to his mom as he paid for nothing.

I moved on with my life, and he stayed in his. He did not work, was a serial cheater, and sometimes watched his daughter when my schedule changed. It hurt my feelings for him to take my daughter around other chicks and their kids. It hurt my feelings being constantly disrespected. It equally hurt my feelings not to feel loved. I still visited my mother and father when I could, but basically, my routine had become work and caring for my daughter.

I was the first of my girlfriends to become a mother. While they were living their lives as college students, partying, experiencing the dating scene and nightlife, I was at home struggling through a poorly structured family relationship. Life was hard, and I fought depression. I had fallen to the wayside of communicating with my sisters. We were all growing up and trying to figure out how to live our lives. When I was not working, I stayed around the house. I did not need a babysitter because I never went anywhere without my child.

One day Coral came to visit with her boyfriend. Despite whispering, William overheard me agree with Coral that her guy was cute. He asked me to come in the back and accused me of flirting. When I laughed it off and told him what happened, he popped me in the mouth and busted my lip.

"What the... Seriously? You're that guy?" I questioned in my head. Up until the 1980s, domestic violence was a private matter, and people rarely got involved in other people's business. I now argue that violence is not a private matter, and battered individuals should have someone to talk to. But at the time, I told Coral she and her boyfriend had to leave, and I escorted them out. She asked if I was okay, and I said yes. I was embarrassed and pissed. This sorry bastard put his hands on me, and I decided then and there he would not kill my spirit.

*****

One day while cleaning up the bedroom, I came across a super family pack of pictures with William, Alicia, some other female, and her children. *How sweet! The loving family portrait I could not get him to sit for with our little family.* My anger and vengefulness returned on high alert. A few times, I would come home from work exhausted and see chicks leave out the front door. I had resigned myself to the abnormalities of this poorly structured family setup, but seeing these pictures was a bit too much. It was like flaunting his audacity in the space I cleaned and found comfort in. Calmly, I tore up the pictures and placed them in his bath towel.

There is something about a hot bath that soothes the mind. Add some bubbles and a cold can of beer, and boom! I had learned how to care for William because he was prone to unusual accidents. Once, he burned his arm up badly in a grease fire. Another time he had a boil or something cut out of his inner butt cheek. Each time, I nursed him back to health.

On this day, I cleaned the bathroom and burned some candles. I ran the water with bubbles and set out the cold beer. After, I went downstairs to the basement and invited him to a comforting bath. I washed his back and pampered him. I made him feel special and offered to dry him off. The look of confusion and then anger when all the torn pictures fell into the sudsy water was priceless. When he realized the pictures were him with the other family, he became angry. I laughed and asked him why he thought I would let that woman take a picture with my child. I left him standing there.

As time passed, living upstairs became intolerable. His mother became contentious, and he started to stay out at night. I started checking pockets and getting disturbed when finding numbers and remnants from other females. The disrespect was gagging.

I began to save money for special occasions to make sure I was covered for celebrations. I bought a special dress and shoes for my first Mother's Day in his mother's home only to be informed that I was not his mother, and there was no reason to celebrate. So, I went out on my own, and as if to make me feel better, his mother let me wear her fur coat. I took my child to visit with Coral and called an ex. I stayed out all night and did not care. William, on the other hand, was angry and embarrassed because his parents came face-to-face with the dysfunction we were living with in their home.

His stepfather looked at me with disdain that Monday morning on his way out to work, and his mother shook her head. It was as if they did not know he was an asshole. Suddenly, I was the bad guy. I left my daughter with Coral because I knew I would have some crap to deal with. My motto is when you fuck up, do it well, and make sure it is worth it. Well, I did, and it was. When I went upstairs, William was emboldened with quiet hostility. He popped me upside the head and left. Disturbed by being struck, again, I straightened up and took a bath. When he returned, he told me that I would be moving in with his grandmother.

"Really, says who?"

"I said so."

"I'm not going."

"Yes, you are because my mom said you can no longer stay here, and you are moving in with my grandmother."

"Nope. You all can put me out, but you can't tell me where to go. We can go to the park and sleep on a bench for all you care, so what difference does it make?"

"You have no place to go."

He was right. I was trapped and seemingly at his mercy, but I did not leave on that day. Eventually, I left, and over time, I hopped from house to house with various family members and saved money to get my own apartment.

Single Parents Struggle

LIFE BECAME MORE PROBLEMATIC. I held on to my job, and my family helped a little. One day, William came to my job and told me he had a place for me to stay. He said the property manager would let him and his brother fix up a building, and then he could have an apartment rent-free. He wanted us to move in. By then, Alicia was two years old. It was February 1982, and I was still gullible. I let this man move me into a fixer-upper without heat. They had painted the walls and cleaned the place. I did not have a refrigerator, so I kept the perishables on the back porch in a cooler with rocks on top in the event an animal was attracted. I tried to make the best of living in a hell hole, but it was nearly impossible.

William eventually put space heaters in the bedroom for warmth, which is where we spent most of our evening time. I realized how bad the situation was when I woke up one morning to the foul smell of molten shit balls. William had put a puppy in the room while we were asleep, and the animal crapped all over the floor in the middle of the night. I woke up to a weeping puppy, a crying baby, and no man. The fear and bravery fought for control of me, and I was stifled, frozen in time, wondering how I had gotten into this hellish predicament called my life. I was confused and bewildered as to how to make the situation any better.

As I walked towards my apartment building the next evening after coming home from work, William's grandmother, who lived next door, opened the window and called me to come in. She had something warm for me to drink, and we settled down. I undressed my daughter from her snowsuit, and she played with her toys left there from previous visits. His grandmother asked me if I lived next door. I put my head down in shame and said yes. She asked why, and I said, "I have no place else to go." She told me I was moving in with her.

"No," I said. "I do not want to be a burden."

"Well, it is too late because I had William bring all your things over. I scolded him for putting you in that building. It is settled; you live here now."

I was tired of fighting alone, so I said okay, lowered my head, and cried. I was humbled by her generosity.

*****

During the time William and I lived with Alicia's great-grandmother, things were somewhat better; however, shortly thereafter, she went to the hospital and never returned. I was told I could stay there but had to pay rent. I thought that was a fair arrangement. William's brother moved in and life with both and their womanly ways became comical. Even though I lived in the apartment and shared a room with William, our relationship was still on the ropes and he ran females in and out while I was at work.

On day while working at the Kentucky Fried Chicken store at 35th in Lake Meadows, I was surprised to see Lance was the next customer in line. I still remembered his order of three wings original and a biscuit with honey. I packed it up, he found a seat in the lobby, and I found time to chat for a few minutes. He was still married, and I in a relationship. Good catching up, Lance; gotta go. But Lance would not leave me alone; he kept popping up at my place of business. I never did find out how he knew where I was. I transferred to a different store, and there he was! I came to expect to see him eventually. On one occasion, he persistently asked to take me home, and I agreed. He parked a few blocks away from my home; we sat in the car in the dark, and then, that kiss. Too much unbridled passion took me to another place of comfort, but it was bad timing. A burn in my belly, a yearning in my thighs, the fear of being busted, and remembering that he was still married brought me to my senses. I got out of the car and walked home.

Back in my reality, my roomie seemed to stop cheating for a while. He started working and bringing home a paycheck. One day, we talked about marriage, and he bought me an engagement ring; however, I never went to get it sized and eventually lost it. When he asked me where the ring was, without remorse, I told him I had lost it. He asked why I did not tell him, and I said I did not know and really didn't care. He appeared to be hurt, but I couldn't have cared any less. We never talked about marriage again.

I came to realize that after all I had endured, I had lost the feeling of needing him. We agreed it was over. My struggle to get to work and care for my child worsened after William and I parted ways. I found an apartment for me and my daughter and even though our relationship had become horrible, he seemed to want to stay with me. The more I resisted, the more combative he became. For a long period, when I did not have a house phone, I would call Serena just to let her know I was okay. Sometimes, she would answer the phone, and I would silently cry into the phone and tell her I made it to work. We had established this protocol because my child's father had become my stalker after I had him forcibly removed from my apartment. How he had gotten back into my life was suspect, as he used the "I'm sorry" trick to convince me he had changed. Since I could always use help, especially from the father, I fell for it and let him move in with us. He was lazy and did not want to work. For instance, before I left for work one day, he asked me if I could take his unemployment worksheet with me and have the managers there fill it out to show he had applied for work. I said, "No, I would not." He asked why, and I stated that I already had a job and did not feel it was my job to lie on his form. He then said, "What if I slammed this refrigerator to the floor? What would you do?" I told him, "I would pick it up, put the meager belongings back on the shelf, and go to work."

When I came home exhausted from work, and he was not there, I would go looking for him and my daughter. Often, he'd be hanging out at Coral and Ruby's house playing cards, smoking weed, and drinking. He always wanted to leave when I got there and expected me to cook and "put out" after I put my daughter down for the night. This routine had become exhausting and chipped away at my sensibilities. I was intimidated by him because, one day, he showed me a gun and put it back in his coat pocket in my hall closet. Another time, he wrote me a chilling letter professing his love for me and what he would do if we ever broke up. I could not figure out how and when he became so "in love" with me and had to figure out a way to get from under him, so I devised a stupid plan.

After work one day, I went to visit Coral and Ruby and told them what was going on, and pulled them in. I invited Ruby and her boyfriend to dinner that night and told her I would swallow some aspirin about an hour before she came, thinking this would be enough time for the medication to kick in. I told her to notice something wrong with me then leave and call 911. I figured when the police arrived and asked what happened, she could tell them that I wanted to be away from him so bad that I was willing to kill myself to be rid of him, then they would arrest him for abuse, and I would be free. My plan failed. I swallowed about 20 aspirins and waited. Ruby and her boyfriend showed up for dinner, and nothing "exciting" happened. Ruby pulled me to the side and asked me if I had taken the pills, and I told her yes. She waited around a little while longer, then she left. Sometime later, I felt nauseous and started cramping. I felt awful and was hugging the toilet with violent convulsions, but nothing came out. I told him to dial 911, and they sent a police wagon to take me to the hospital. I told the nurse what I had done, and she was troubled and asked why. I told her I was in an abusive relationship and was scared to leave. I told her I thought this was the only way I could think to get away from him. She left to write up the report. He later came back to visit, and as if someone told him what I had said, he leaned over the bed to my ear and whispered, "If you tell anyone anything bad about me, I will kill you." I said, "Okay."

The nurse came back with a black liquid and told me to drink it. I asked her what it was, and she said it would cause me to vomit. She then told me that if I did not throw up, my kidneys would fail, and if I threw up, they could be made stronger. The nurse said if I resisted, they would force the liquid and admit me to the psychiatric ward for counseling. I learned then that I did not have the right to take my own life. While I knew I was not crazy, and some counseling would do me good, I also knew I had to care for my daughter, so I drank the thick, black liquid charcoal. I threw up immediately. After a while, I was admitted into the hospital, and for the first time in months, I slept with ease. I woke up in a private room and bright sunlight, only to be darkened with his presence and more threats. When he left, I told the nurse to refuse all visitors, as if I would get any visitors. I was too embarrassed to tell anyone I was there. I left the hospital on the second day and went home to him still in my apartment and making demands. I told myself to take deep breaths. *Val, you can get out of this nightmare.*

As the New Year approached, I was finally fed up and devised another plan to get rid of William. I was working regularly and taking care of my responsibilities while he was still a controlling, abusive asshole. So, I flipped the script and started pretending I loved him and wanted to make it work. After a couple of weeks, I was off work and decided I would not bring in the New Year with this albatross around my neck. The next morning, I showered, dressed, stuck my lease agreement in my pant pocket, and dressed my little girl. I told him we were going to the store to buy the groceries for breakfast, and I was taking "our" daughter so that she could pick whatever she wanted from the store as a treat. I took my daughter around the corner to my sister's place, went to a payphone, and called the police. I told them I had an unwanted person in my home, and he was abusive. I waited across the street from my building in front of Walgreens until they arrived. When the police car pulled up, I went over and told them who I was. I escorted them to my apartment, opened the door, and we all entered the tiny hallway. I pointed him out and said, "That's him! I want him out of here!" Shocked, he lunged at me, and I hid behind the police and shouted, "Don't let him touch me!" The female officer was responsive; however, the male officer said to him when he asked what was going on, "Awe, it's just a li'l domestic dispute; she'll be alright." When the abuser stated it was his apartment as well, I pulled out my lease and proved his name was not on it. They allowed him to get dressed, then handcuffed him, and escorted him out. I told them to wait so I could give them the gun, but it was gone. Damn! Physical evidence would have been good.

I waited a few minutes, then got on a bus and went to another sister's house further away to wait it out. I then called the sisters who were watching my daughter, and they reported that he had come by earlier with his brother wielding a shotgun demanding to know where I was. I asked them in a shaking voice where my child was, and they said they hid the kids in a closet when they saw him from the front window. He left the message that I was going to pay for the disrespect. I called the police and reported the incident and added to the quickly growing report. I was told an arrest warrant would be put out for him and that he was considered armed and dangerous. I stayed out of my apartment for about a week because I could not find my door keys. I shuffled my daughter back and forth between my sisters' households so my abuser could not find her.

After about a week, I walked to the bus to visit my friend Lance since Alicia had a playdate with his daughter Patricia that day. As I approached the bus stop, I saw two guys who were boyfriends of Coral and Ruby standing together near the bus stop with my ex. I was scared at the sight of him, and he lunged. They held him back, and I hollered, "Hold him, the bus is coming!" I jumped on the bus hurriedly asked the driver just to take off as he was trying to board the bus. I got off the bus several stops later, walked the few blocks to Lance's house, and rang the doorbell. He immediately asked me what was wrong. In a shaky voice, I told him what had just happened. We went downstairs where the girls were playing, and I watched him go in the safe and pull out his gun. I asked him what it was for, and he said he was going to handle it. I asked him not to and convinced him it would be alright. This was not his fight.

The following day, I had the building landlord make me a new set of keys after changing the locks. I was finally able to enter my apartment. Someone had been in my apartment, and I suspected it was my ex because there was an eerie message scratched in my headboard stating he loved my daughter and me, filled in with red nail polish. I searched but could not find the threatening letter he had written and mailed to me.

Weeks went by, and I knew he was following me because I would see him duck into hallways or hide behind street corners. The hair would raise on the back of my neck when he was near, yet nothing was heard from him until one day, he called me at work just before quitting time. He said he wanted to see me, and I said, "No, thank you." He started with the threats of violence and false statements of love. I told him he was a liar, cheat, weak, and I hurled upon him indignities and insults; the fear had vanished. I would no longer be held hostage to his tirades. I would no longer look over my shoulder, waiting for him to pounce. I was tired of his bullshit and was ready to end it, one way or the other. I told him to come to pick me up from work at five. Skeptical, he asked me why?

"Do you want me to take you to the bank?"

"No, come get me at 5:30," I said. "That way, I'll be finished counting down my drawers."

"Why? What do you want?"

"Motherfucker, one of us is gonna die today, and if it's me, I'm taking some of yo' pretty ass with me."

I hung up the phone then went into my purse. I pulled out the bag of disposable razors, burst it open, broke the plastic, and removed the blades. I looked in the drawer and searched for the Scotch tape, then I taped the razors, blade side up, between the top of my fingers. I wrote down two phone numbers on a piece of paper, gave it to the head cashier, and told her if anything happened to me, dial 911, then call the two numbers. I told her the first was my family, and the second was his mother. I placed a sharp knife behind the front counter. I gathered my belongings and waited. After about 2 hours, I realized he was not coming. I caught the bus and went home; I had won this round. Several days later, I got a call from another store stating someone left a set of keys at the drive-thru window. I asked the caller to describe the keys, and I realized they were mine. I smiled and relaxed, knowing he would finally leave me alone. After all the fighting, stalking, abuse, chipping away at my self-esteem, hindering me from growing as a woman and a mother, and the depression I had endured, I felt relieved. Through the sacrifices, desperation for family, and the longing to provide a two-parent household for my child, I had fallen in love and become a parent with the wrong man. He was not for me, and I finally realized the importance of being safe. I moved on in my endeavors of being a loving and supportive mother to my child, still not knowing or having a plan for the end game or future goals.

Alicia was almost three years old, and I was still employed with the same fast-food company. I worked hard and spent my off days with my daughter. Some of my other sisters lived in the same neighborhood, so they took turns babysitting for pay. Things seemed to be working out.

After saving my portion, my sister Amber and I decided to live together. Living with Amber was cool. We both worked for the same fast-food company but in different stores and opposite shifts. Our apartment only had one bedroom and an additional bed for Alicia, off the kitchen. We managed to get along well, as we mostly passed each other coming and going, but during the times we were together, Amber and I became very close. Though she was five years my junior, we had enough in common, that we gelled well. My two best friends Serena and Vivian also came around a lot but not as much as the sisters who watched Alicia. It seemed we had mostly a business relationship instead of a family bond. It did not make matters any better with our mother moving first out of state and then to Monrovia, Liberia, Africa with my two youngest sisters Jasmine and Beryl. My mother's absence was a heavy burden for me since I needed her for advice and support. To make up for her absence, I forged a relationship with William's mother. She and I got along well enough if boundaries were not crossed. I must admit she was more for her son than me, and when necessary, she tended to see his way instead of the right way. Nevertheless, we had a relationship, and I could go to his side of the family for some modicum of support when needed.

Considering the many challenges I faced, there came a time when, for some reason, my sisters did not feel like watching Alicia. I was in a bind and needed immediate help. I had a nephew who seemed to be a sweet young boy, and as a family, we were all close and knew each other's children quite well. Even though my sister Opal lived on the west side of Chicago, my nephew was always on the south side around us, and we all had a loving relationship with him. I asked him to watch my daughter for a few weeks until I could make other arrangements. I didn't want to take up too much of his time because most teenagers typically don't want to be stuck with little kids. We worked out a schedule and agreed on a small pay, and I was able to work my night shifts with ease.

After a few weeks of this setup, I was surprised to hear my doorbell ring at around 7 p.m. It was Opal. I buzzed her in, and she came upstairs. When she came in, she looked at her son and said, "So you over here now, huh?" She had a bewildered look on her face, and he suddenly looked scared. I asked her what was going on, and she responded with the frightening news.

Opal had been going to family court because her son had molested his younger sister and two younger brothers. I gasped! I put my hand over my heart as it started to pound in my chest!

"Wait," I said. "What do you mean he's been molesting your younger kids?"

She told me she had been to court on two occasions without him, and the judge told her today that she only had one more chance to appear in court without him by her side. If her son did not come to the next court hearing, the judge would take her other children away. Horrible!

I could hardly form words, then I said, "But you've been here for two weeks watching my child! Oh my god, have you touched my child?" He said no, but I could not believe him. It was a nightmare. I looked at my darling sweet baby and wondered if she had been touched. I looked up and told him he had to go. He attempted to plead with me that his mother would beat him.

I said, "So?! You have to go!" He gathered his things, and they left.

Stunned, I picked up my little girl and guided her to the couch. She was young and innocent, and I did not know what to do next. She seemed alright every night I came home. I never noticed anything different when I bathed her. She did not wear Pampers, and he did not have to dress her, so I assumed everything was okay. A few minutes later, the doorbell rang again. Opal was back. She said as soon as they got outside, her son ran. Bewildered, I got my little girl, and we went to bed. I had her sleep with me.

Admittedly, I felt awful and betrayed by the sudden turn of events. I thought my sister should have come around sooner and told us what was going on in her home, especially since she had said she figured he was hanging out with us. She stated she had looked for him and then realized he must be on the south side with her sisters, so since children were at stake, she would come and check it out. I wondered again if he had touched my child. I looked for evidence and thought back to how she was behaving and concluded she was okay. I thought that was the appropriate response, especially since I had never experienced anything of this magnitude.

The next morning, I went about my business as usual with my daughter. When it was time for work, we went the few blocks to my sisters' house, where Coral and Ruby lived, and I asked them to watch Alicia until I could make other arrangements. After they said yes, I sat down for a quick chat. I asked them if Opal had come by and given them the rundown on her son. They said yes, but they did not believe her.

"Why not?" I asked.

"Because everybody knows she's crazy and makes shit up."

"Why would she lie about her own child and say something so ugly?" I challenged.

No response.

"Well, I don't want him to watch my child ever again! Please do not have him watch her when you all leave. Just watch her please because I must work," I pleaded.

I went to work confident that my sisters would do as I said and not let our molesting nephew watch any of our children, especially mine, ever again. As time went by, I settled back into my routine, working hard to meet some goal I could not quite put my finger on. I just knew I was supposed to work and take care of my daughter and do my best to provide and keep her safe. I had a little fun; my friends sometimes visited when they were free, and time moved on. I did not have an end game or a goal in mind. I just kept moving forward.

LIFE CAME TO A HALT!

IN FEBRUARY OF 1983, I graduated from Chicken College and earned a certificate of completion. I became an Assistant Manager! I learned how to be reliable and proficient, and I was willing to work at several stores. I was being trained for management and aspired to run my own store one day. I dug in my heels and learned the trade. I learned what to do when winter storms made the pipes freeze or when rainy days caused floods in the lobby. Not running out of chicken and side dishes during the rush hour and finding the right tone when customers complained became my strengths. I learned to order supplies according to daily sales and perform store inventory audits. All aspects of management were important to succeed in the business. I took my job seriously and was committed to being a success story for my family.

One winter evening, we did not have running water in the store. The cooks had to fill buckets with snow, bring them in, and heat to a boil. The hot water cleaned the grease from the floors and washed the dishes. It took all night to clean the store before we could leave. The sun had risen, and the morning crew was checking in to start their shift when we could finally leave. As I walked from corner to corner to stave off the cold air before the bus arrived, the liquid grease on my pants hardened and stuck to my knees. Sometimes, I walked from the store on 83rd and Jeffery to 71st and Jeffery before a bus came around 2 a.m. or 3 a.m. I would arrive home exhausted, only to awaken a few hours later to spend time with my daughter before going back to work. This had become my workday routine. When possible, I scheduled two days off to spend time with Alicia and then find some time for myself. On a few occasions, William would ask for her over the weekend but did not have the means to provide for her. I would pack her bag with breakfast and snacks and give him a little cash. I did not want his lack of money to prevent her from spending time with him. I let the routine play out until I could no longer tolerate the disrespect of him not being where we agreed for pickup and his lack of concern for wasting my precious time.

His inconsiderate ways pushed me to my limits one Saturday when I was scheduled to pick up my little girl. I caught the bus and rode across town to his place, and he was not there. His roommate said his mother had come to visit, and without telling me, the three of them left. I was quickly irritated after getting little sleep so I could be on time, only for him to have left. I caught the bus to Coral's home and called his mother's house. She answered the phone and was instantly rude and hung up. I called back, and no one answered. I was pissed. I caught the bus home and called again. This time William answered, and I snapped off. He hung up, and I called right back and was told that unless I learned to speak to him with respect, he would not talk to me. Indignation swelled up in me, and I ran off a litany of who the hell did he think he was talking to.

"You black motherfucker! If it were not for me, you would not even know your daughter, let alone be able to spend time with her!"

He hung up again. I called one more time and told him to bring my daughter home. He refused and repeated that I had to learn to respect him. Furious, I called the police and explained my problem. Since his mother lived in a different police district, I was advised to go to the public phone on 76th Cottage Grove and call back using a reference number. When I called back, a police car came to pick me up to get my child. He asked me who had custody, and I told him I did. When asked for papers, I could not produce any. He told me that possession is 9/10th of the law, and either of us could have her until a court said differently. Seeing my distress, he said that he would try to help me and drove me to his mother's house.

I realized I was in unchartered territory but anxiously tried to exit the car when I saw my daughter in the back seat of the car that was driving behind us. The officer told me to wait and to let him handle it. When he went to the house and spoke with the grandparents, William came up, heard what was going on, then came to the car. He threw her bag of clothes in my face and told me I could have my child and to stay the hell away from him.

I said, "Fine with me," and smiled. The police officer brought Alicia to the car, and all was well in the world again.

As a single parent, you learn to endure, sacrifice, and do your best by any means necessary for your children. I struggled with one child, so I could not imagine having multiple children. I admired the women who worked, went to school, and took care of their children alone. Mothers work hard, deal with sexual harassment from men and women who want to lie with them, and for the sake of survival, some run drugs, work at strip clubs, or worse, prostitute themselves. I chose the fast-food environment to make honest money. I had to learn to ignore the catcalls from the men in the street. You look the other way at the laughs from those who say you smell like the food you work around or mock the ugly uniform you wear. You learn to hold your head high when called a chicken queen or a burger flipper. Insults are insults, but the beauty is knowing what your battles are and how and when to fight them. I was employed, and my child had everything she needed. She was being provided for in my absence by loving people who also wanted what was best for her.

Unfortunately, working around money lures undesirables to the work-place. Robberies seemed commonplace, and police responses were pathetic. While working at one store on Stony Island, two guys came in just before closing. There was approximately fifteen dollars in the drawer and little to no food for sale. I had done a good job with time management by sending some employees home early and keeping waste low. When one of the two men ordered their food, the other pulled out a gun and said he wanted what was in the drawers. I showed him how little was there, and he demanded I open the safe. So, I spun the dial and set the timer to open and told him it would take a few minutes. They were not the smartest criminals, which allowed me and the other cashier to constantly press the police alarm. They eventually got tired of waiting, paid for their food, then took all the money, including theirs, and left. The police answered the alarm about thirty minutes later, and I filed a report. The area manager stated I had wasted her time because she had to come to the store, and since the amount that was stolen was so small, I should not have called the police. On the other hand, I thought I was being efficient by following the appropriate process for a robbery. Besides, how else was I supposed to explain the missing cash?

On another occasion, at the 35th Street location in the Lake Meadows strip mall, this young man, who I recognized as a regular, attempted to rob the store with an empty wine bottle. I laughed at him and told him that he should at least break off the neck and threaten me with sharp glass. In his frustration of not evoking fear in me, he threw the wine bottle. I ducked and came back up with a dishpan full of water. I threw that at him, and he ran out of the store. I filed a police report and was scolded again. This time, my carelessness of throwing a metal object could have shattered the glass window—a valid point.

There was a time at another store on 43rd in Indiana when I could not rid the store of gang members. The store was in the heart of the hood, surrounded by many businesses and foot traffic. The area attracted those who hustled to make their money legitimately and illegitimately. The store got crowded in the early mornings to feed those with drinking problems looking to buy a piece of chicken with a biscuit, "working women" coming off the night shift, and juvenile delinquents. They would come into the store and harass the other customers. I knew calling the police would make matters worse, so I would grit my teeth and deal with it.

One evening on the way home, I saw a young girl that I recognized across the street and invited her into my place. The apartment building she was near was not a place for young girls, and I told her that people who hung around that location were trouble. She told me she was living there. I was alarmed and convinced her to spend the night. The next morning, after I fixed her breakfast, I called the police and reported a runaway. I believed it was the right thing to do because she was not safe. When the police came to get her, she became hysterical and scratched up my face and arms in her struggle to avoid being handcuffed. I cried as they took her away and hoped they'd take her to her mother since I knew who she was.

When I got to work the next day, a man came in, ordered his food, and thanked me for calling the police that morning. I asked why, and he stated that it was his daughter who had run away from home. She had been missing for several weeks. He then turned around and looked at the gang members and told them that from then on out, they were to leave me and my store alone. He told them to empty the garbage and do anything else that I asked them. He told me he was their leader. Instant relief and appreciation enveloped me, which only lasted for a few weeks, as he was murdered shortly afterward while sitting in a car across the street.

Single Parent Baby Steps

.

Single parents struggle in a different way than married women. I had money and could sustain what I assumed was enough, though I didn't have the slightest vision of where my life would guide me or what was in store: my immediate concern was survival and maintainability. I always thought myself to be an attractive female, but that did not seem to amount to much. Looks did not pay the bills, nor did looks provide for my child. Let us be clear though, men did try to get with me, but for some reason, it did not matter. The survival of an abusive relationship that had the potential to end my life was enough by itself.

Being in bars and around men was still a foreign concept to me, as if I had been living in a sheltered environment for years and had missed the women's revolution. I timidly explored the nightlife and realized it was not really for me since I had too many trust issues and was afraid of getting close to men. One-night stands and feeling like I was a piece of meat did not interest me, and if this was the great hoorah, I wanted no parts of it.

But then, while riding the bus one day on my way to work, I began to notice a lot of attractive men. "*Wait, who is that? Wow, he looks good! Where did all these good-looking men come from?*" I wondered. I asked Serena, and she said they had always been here.

"But how?" I asked. I had never seen them. She told me that I was too deep in my relationship to notice other guys. She said I was blind to what else was out there. Amazing!

I started dating for the first time in my adult life, and it was fun. It was a candy shop. So many eligible men, and *I was single.* I started fitting guys into my day. I flirted at work. I accepted dinner dates and had a steady guy to take care of my womanly needs. Though I was having lots of fun, no one ever met my daughter. Dating was a juggling act because having a guy over meant I had to seek childcare outside of the home. It seemed like I had been in a relationship forever, so I took the time and dated a variety of men. I made sure I dated different types of men to gauge what I liked and what I did not have tolerance for. Roughnecks, salty attitudes, quick tempers, and selfish behaviors were definite turn offs. If the guy had children, he had to be accountable; however, I was only attracted to unattached men. When asked why I never asked for money for my child, I replied, "I work to take care of her. I do not take, need, or want any guy's money. Taking money comes with a price, and we are not for sale." My daughter's needs were never on the table for discussion.

If it had not been for my relationships with Vivian and Serena, I would not have been able to endure abandonment by my mother, attempted molestation, being beaten by my siblings, street fighting, and heartbreak. And while we didn't see each other as often as we had during our teen years, I was still close with both of them. I was able to visit Vivian anytime I wanted. She had married, had children, and was doing domestic things. My visits always rewarded me with the surprise of another child, whom she would never tell me about. I always enjoyed our visits and loved her dearly. While we never ventured outside of her home, what I needed from her was the look of love and acceptance in her eyes and her gentle smile. She would always tell me I could do better when it came to my ex, and I always asked how.

On the other hand, I could not readily visit Serena because she lived so far south, and at the time, I was not familiar with the trains going in her direction. However, by the time I was single, I became more adventurous and would meet up with her and other friends from our school days to eat out, go shopping, or go to the movies. I felt the most liberated when I ventured out publicly without my daughter. Sitting around sipping wine and talking idly was refreshing. Serena never failed to stay in touch with me by coming to my home and taking me out for dinner. She was my hero, and her love and acceptance of the little girl from the projects warmed my heart. She, too, gave me the best advice even though she had never had to endure my atrocities. She gave me hope and never questioned our friendship. Both of my friends came when I called and supported me without question. I could not depend on my sisters for this level of loyalty. I had come to garner serious trust issues with my sisters, which prevented me from sharing my horrors as a young woman.

Some of my horrors included working until the early mornings, taking public transportation home, and being treated like a prostitute, maybe because I was out so late at night on 63rd Street, which was the stomping ground for working women. One early morning, a "pimped out Cadillac" on 63rd Street blocked my passage, and the driver, looking like a damn fool, got out and tried to coerce me into driving away with him. As I kept walking past him, he said, "Girl, you too pretty to be out here wearing a chicken uniform. Come work for me, and you can make some real money." After telling him I was not interested and rushing past him, he stopped. However, he accosted me several more times before he left me alone.

In fact, many men and women attempted to pick me up. Seemingly ordinary men harassed me, and their girlfriends wanted to fight me because their boyfriends tried to talk to me while they watched. With the stores I worked in always being robbed, Lance's girlfriend constantly popping by and either trying to be my friend or looking for him after they had argued, William's bullshit, and needing my mother, it was more than enough to make me break down.

The struggles of being a single mother became the driver of the bus in my life. The routine of getting up, providing for my daughter, taking her to the sitter and going to work kept me grounded. The comfort of knowing my daughter would have no reason to question my love, loyalty, and sacrifices for her as I had with my mother was my secret prayer. I could not imagine having to answer the question, "mama, where were you?" as I often wondered of my mother. One of my biggest fears was not being able to keep the lights on or not having snacks during the day. In fact, I made sure Alicia had a plethora of clothes, including a pair of cowboy boots, because I thought they were too cute and a must-have.

My goal was to make sure she would never look unkept. I spoiled her and wanted to make up for the material things I did not have as a child. To me that meant having a lot of toys, taking her out to restaurants and the movies, and celebrating holidays. And while I did not have fashion sense for myself, my little one was always dressed in the latest styles for girls with her hair combed and looking perfect. To me, this was evidence of doing something worthwhile and right. I did not think anyone could ever question my parenting skills based on my daughter's appearance and happy demeanor. These little things pushed me to work and be disciplined as I persevered in hopes of one day finding my place in life and society.

THE FIGHT FOR MY LIFE!

APRIL 17, 1984, WAS a dreary day. The sky was overcast and there was a drizzle of rain. I went to my sister's house that late afternoon to drop off my daughter and visit with my nephew because he was scheduled to have ear surgery. After I cuddled and loved him for a while, I left to work the closing shift from 5 p.m. to 2 a.m. I had scheduled my favorite two closers and anticipated an easy evening.

When I arrived at the store, I checked in and started my shift. Foot traffic was about normal, and the team worked as expected. We joked in our usual way as the evening drifted through the late night. The head cook was new to the team, as he had just requested to work nights two weeks earlier to earn more money because his girlfriend was expecting their first child. He and I had worked on some day shifts in the past, and I found him to be 'mostly' reliable and skilled in his tasks. He kept the food coming, worked without attitude, and was easy to get along with. Working with him had always been effortless. The head cashier was also reliable, dependable, and skilled on the front counter. There were two additional personnel working with us. The second cashier was new to the team and needed guidance since she was still in training, while the second cook had been onboard for several months but lacked the skillset to be the head cook. I had two skilled people on hand, which should have made it an unproblematic night at work.

As the sun set and the sky darkened, I turned on the outside lights. They illuminated the property from the front peninsula and back garbage dumpster to each street surrounding the building. The store faced Jeffery Blvd. and was sided by 83rd Street to the right and South Chicago on the left, all streets running two lanes of traffic.

Ordinarily, the evening shift was busy and hectic because of the store's location, but due to the weather, the foot traffic into the store slowed remarkably as the evening lingered. At the drive-thru, a customer told me that it was dark around the store, so he did not realize the store was open. So, I went to make sure the lights were on, and the switch was in the upright position; it was. Without realizing the store was still surrounded by darkness, I continued to work my shift. Later, another customer walked in and scolded me for not turning on the outside lights. I looked out the window and saw the company's marquee on the tall pole was lit up. The customer then said, "Yeah, but it's dark everywhere else." In a confused state, I called the area manager and explained the situation so she could come over and investigate. I had worked for this area manager in all the stores over the past four years. As usual, once she fixed the problem, she accused me of being inefficient. She said somehow the electric panel had been accessed, and all the switches were in the off position, so she turned them back on. She informed me that she expected me to be more cognizant of duties and that I had to learn all aspects of running a store if I aspired to be a store manager. She then performed a cursory audit of the store and advised me on how to adjust activities when business slowed so that I would not waste product. It was good advice, and I stored the knowledge.

As the evening dragged on, another drive-thru customer told me the lights were off again, and my stress level increased. Since it was near to closing time, I did not bother to reset the panel. A little while later, after they had completed their tasks, I let the second cashier and second cook out the front door while the other cashier, cook, and I proceeded to clean up for the night. About an hour later, the head cashier was ready to go, and the cook said he would let her out as I was at the sink washing his dishes. For some reason, on this night, he was moving unusually slow in his duties because, typically, we would all leave together. As I saw him follow her out the front of the store, I noticed how he changed his anticipated path to the sink and went around towards the fryers to the back door. I heard the back door open and suddenly thought, *Why would he open the back door? He knows that's a safety risk.* I shook my head and proceeded to wash the dishes, then looked up to my right and saw a strange man pointing a gun in my face. The cook rushed up and said, "Val, we gotta do everything these guys say. They mean business!"

I thought, *What guys? All I see is you and him.*

The gunman pointed towards the back office and directed me to move, so I did. As we neared the back office where the desk was, the man with the gun instantly touched my right hand as if to stop me from pushing the alarm concealed near the drawer.

I thought, *How did he know the alarm was there?*

The gunman told me the store is being robbed, and he wanted me to open the safe. I told him the safe was behind the counter. He directed me by gunpoint to walk towards the front of the store where the safe was located. The head cook walked behind me and started mumbling with fear in his voice, saying, "Do what they say; they mean business." I was very confused as to what role he was playing. I kept looking around for another guy, and the gunman told me to face front.

Once at the safe, he patted my hands again, noting where the alert button was, and again, I wondered how he knew the details of the store. My hands shook as I attempted to spin the dial to unlock the timer on the safe. After getting the combination wrong twice, he told me that I had better get it right or else. The cook said, "Val, calm down, you can do this. I don't wanna get shot."

I thought, *Who's gonna shoot you? Aren't you in on this?*

I finally opened the safe, and the gunman was pissed because the only cash was four drawers with $40 in each. I told him that tonight's money was in a separate compartment, and the timer was on a 10-minute delay. He told me to start the timer. While I kneeled on the floor, I noticed the gunman waving the pistol as he talked to his "friend." I saw the cook motion him to keep the weapon low to prevent people outside from seeing what was going on inside as they drove or walked past the drive-thru window from the other side of the residential street. I was then directed to the walk-in refrigerator with the gun stuck in my lower back.

As I stood in the walk-in, I heard banging sounds in the kitchen. I heard coins being shuffled, cash drawers being dropped on the metal sinks, and two distinct voices—the cook and the gunman. The gunman came in the walk-in with the gun pointing at me. Fear and anxiety crept up my stomach to my chest and throat. Apprehension and a disquieting humiliation swept over me as he looked down my blouse. I started to sweat when he told me to stand in the corner.

While walking to the corner, I looked over my left shoulder and asked, "You're not gonna hurt me, are you?"

He said, "Naw baby, I just don't want you to see me leave." I turned to look at the wall corner; then, I looked over my right shoulder. I saw the gun in his right hand, pointing towards the floor. I saw blue smoke emanating from the gun's nozzle and smelled gun powder. I looked back at the corner wall and saw myself fall to the floor in slow motion. I looked to my left, and the gunman was gone. When I landed on the floor, I waited for a beat or two, then tried to get up. My body and head felt heavy. I saw a pool of blood under me and thought I must have hit my head on the trays on my way down. I slumped back down on the floor and waited. An unexpected wave of exhaustion shrouded me, and I closed my eyes to sleep, rationalizing the morning manager could wake me.

Abruptly, a gush of cold air covered my face from the freezer a few feet in front of me. My eyes popped open, and I said to myself, "My daughter's birthday is in ten days; I gotta get up!"

I sluggishly stood up with my head to my chest as blood dripped down the right side of my face. Walking towards the door, the left side of my neck felt swollen, and I struggled to keep my head straight. Excruciating pain throbbed in my head as I recounted the situation before me. I slowly opened the door to hear if the robbers were still in the store while simultaneously pushing the alarm. I suddenly remembered all the other times when one of the stores was robbed and knew time was not my friend. I decided to push the button as if I knew emergency signals; I needed the police to take this robbery seriously and come now.

*****

Absorbed with anxiety, I opened the door, wondering if my assailants were still in the store. At a snail's pace, I let my head drop to my chest and managed to make it to the front to see if anyone was in the store. I noticed the empty drawers and safe. I checked to see if the robbers were hiding in the bathrooms and found no one, then I walked back to the office. I noticed the back door in the kitchen was cracked open and decided to close it. The closer I got to the door, the more I realized I had not checked the floor in front of the salad case on the lobby side; they could have been hiding there waiting to attack me. I closed the door with the anticipated slam and waited for their surprise appearance. My fear increased as I walked to the office and dialed 911, then Amber, then a guy friend I was to visit that night.

I told the 911 operator my name, the store's address and reported the store had been robbed. I also told them that my head hurt badly because I must have bumped it on my fall to the floor or that I might have been shot in the head. Amber told me later that I said I had been shot in the head, and I needed her to meet me at the hospital. She said she thought it was a bad joke, but then I repeated, "I've been shot in the head" with an attitude. I hung up the phone and walked to the front door. I forgot my purse and leather jacket so I walked back to the office.

As I walked back towards the front of the store for the second time, the phone rang, and it was the store manager. I told him what happened and who I suspected and hung up. Again, I started walking to the front of the store, and the phone rang. It was the area manager, and she was pissed. She told me she was tired of my theatrics. I screamed and told her to call the store manager and hung up! I finally reached the front of the store where police were now banging on the drive-thru and front door windows. I opened the door, told the officer who did it then fainted.

I woke up in the back of a police car with a barrage of questions thrown at me. I tried to answer but was stricken with a punishing headache. I did not understand why my head was hurting or why blood was slowly dripping down my face. It wasn't easy to keep my head straight while it lobbed back and forth. I asked them to please tell me why my head hurt so much, and they said they did not know. They said an ambulance was on the way and asked me to be a little more patient.

Sometime later, I heard the sirens from the ambulance and was assisted out of the car. I suddenly lost it. I started screaming and waving my arms frantically and crying uncontrollably. I was confused and did not know what was happening to me or why. I begged for someone to please help me understand what was going on. I was told to walk up the stairs and was instructed to sit up instead of lie down on the metal table. I needed rest and was exhausted. As I gripped the rails and tried to hold my balance, the ambulance sped to South Shore Community Hospital.

When I arrived at the hospital, I was put in a wheelchair and rolled to the emergency area. Someone helped me take off my clothes and put on a hospital gown. A nurse took my vitals while I sat on the side of the bed. The area manager was there, and she appeared concerned. Someone took me to get an x-ray; I was cold and uncomfortable. They told me to lie flat the first time, then turn to my side, then I was instructed to lie on my back. The pain was horrendous. The hammer was pounding inside my head. I could not relate to this level of discomfort.

After they sat me up and put me back in the wheelchair, someone came in and said, "Wait, we need x-rays of her head."

I cursed loudly as they guided me back to the table. The depths of cold made me shiver from my toes to the top of my head, but I tried to lay still for more pictures. Finally, they had enough images, and I was wheeled back to the bed. This time, I was able to sit up and lie back in the bed for comfort after I was layered with hot blankets. A nurse asked me if I wanted someone to come and hold my hand. I was surprised to learn so many people had come to see me. In fact, my sister had called everyone, and all my siblings were in the waiting room, some causing a ruckus for not knowing what was going on.

A short while later, the doctor and my sister Amber came towards my bed in unison. The doctor told me that I had been shot in the head with a .22 caliber pistol at close range, one centimeter from my spine. Any closer, and I could have been paralyzed for life. He said that the bullet shattered into multiple pieces. Three to four of those fragments were wedged in the base of my skull at the entry site, and several more were floating around in my head. He said that they had to wait to see where those fragments would land before further diagnoses could be assessed.

Not believing what I had already suspected, I asked incredulously, "What do you mean, I've been shot in the head? I can think. I can walk. We are having this conversation. The cook let his friend in the back door of the store around 11:15 p.m. I was guided to the front of the store at gunpoint.

The gunman put me in the walk-in fridge and later came back, robbed me, and then told me to stand in the corner. Everything was over around 11:37 p.m. How could I have been shot, and I remember all of this?" I fainted. Sometime later, they told me I was to be admitted to the hospital for observation. I felt defeated and confused. Amber told me our brother Clay was there. I asked if he could go up to the room with me and they said yes. I had not seen Clay in six months because he and I had a big argument. I remember it all being my fault and hoped he was not still angry and would not mind escorting his little sister up to her hospital room. When I arrived in my room, someone put a foam brace around my neck then propped me up in the bed. My brother kissed me on the forehead and left the room. My last memory for the night was the nurse asking me who he was to me because he was so handsome. I told her he was my brother and happily married. I thanked God for my life and fell asleep.

*****

Wide awake with a pounding headache, I was in a sit-up position in the hospital the next morning. I was fearful of my next move after being told not to fully lay down, which may have further complicated my condition. Within minutes after waking up, a rush of people surrounded me; doctors, nurses, family members, and the area manager who became a constant presence in the hospital over the next five days. The most unusual sight was Opal, who came into the room, held my foot, and prayed silently. She later inquired whether I had crossed over and met with God. When I told her no, she did not believe me. Over the years, I was able to convince her that no such meeting took place; however, she informed me that I was her miracle story in her church circle.

Remarkably, while in my room, the next five days were filled with many pleasant visitors praying for a speedy recovery. Amber told me she was receiving violent, threatening phone calls from my assailants and their girlfriends. We were scared, and I was worried because I had recently cashed my first big IRS refund check, and it was in the house. I called Lance to ask him if he could meet up with one of my sisters and put the money in his safe. Yet, when I spoke with him on the phone, he was confused because he had heard that I was dead.

I laughingly responded, "No, silly, I'm not dead; I've been shot in the head." Lance showed up on day three after I spoke with him. He did only one thing after he kissed me on the forehead; he kneeled and held my right hand for hours. I found Lance's stay at the hospital unsettling because he was separated from his wife and he had a girlfriend. I assumed the girlfriend would be pissed if she knew he was spending hours visiting me. During his visit, he held my hand long enough to annoy me. When a security guard came to question the presence of my many visitors and asked to see their passes, I told him "*this guy did not have a pass,*" and Lance was asked to leave. The look on his face conveyed hurt and sadness.

Most bothersome the first few days was the constant ringing in my left ear. This was good news to the doctors as they were patiently waiting to see where the floating bullet fragments would land. When I told the nurse that the constant ringing was nerve-shattering, another CT SCAN revealed the fragments were near my left inner ear and were responsible for the vibration and ringing sounds. I went into surgery and had the fragments removed. The doctors were confident I was out of the woods and on to a speedy recovery, as it appeared all my faculties were intact.

During my hospital stay, two detectives came by, and in private, I identified my assailants from a picture line up. The detectives went to their homes and questioned them.

The cook's response when asked the last time he saw me was, "After she let me out the store and locked the door." He and his accomplice, the shooter, were arrested and charged with armed robbery and attempted murder. Shortly after their arrest, Amber started receiving death threats and was warned what would happen to both of us if I testified. I reported the threats to the police, and it was handled. Three months later, they each pleaded guilty and were sentenced to fifteen years for each crime concurrently. Lance called me on the fourth day and insisted on taking me home once I was released, and I told him that he could. He never showed up, so the area manager instead took me home. I left the hospital after five days, then the real nightmares began.

RECOVERY IS SCARY

BEFORE I COULD SETTLE comfortably into my recovery, my employers had arranged for me to be evaluated by a psychologist, who suggested I schedule to return to work quickly. He thought that using the military rationale for pilots was in order: The theory was that if I went back to work quickly, as a pilot who was shot down in his plane, I would not have time to develop fears, as the pilot would not have time to become fearful of flying. That sounded reasonable, and I scheduled a return-to-work date.

As the day of my return neared, I became excited and anxious. In preparation for the big day, I tried on my uniform and looked in the mirror. I expected to see a well-fitted uniform, but my clothes had become too big. I had not noticed the weight loss over the few short weeks. As I tucked my shirt tighter in my pants, I happened to look up and wipe what I thought was blood from my brow. Confused, I looked at my hand; it was wet but not red. It was sweat. I looked in the mirror and adjusted my hat, but it became too tight, so I snatched it from my head. I started sweating profusely, and my throat tightened. My shirt collar was too small, and my fingers fumbled as I tried to loosen the knot on my tie. It felt like someone had struck me with fire!

My eyes burned from the sweat, and tears formed in my eyes. The hallway got hotter, and I panicked. I was suffocating and struggled to catch my breath. As my heart raced, I wondered if I was having a heart attack. I was so frightened and alone in the tiny hall. I spread my arms for balance and buckled towards the floor. I leaned up against the door with my knees to my chest and tried to contain the fear of seeing myself in uniform for the first time since the robbery. Frightened, alone, and afraid of everything, I turned down to the floor, prayed for strength, and cried for what seemed like hours.

Amber came home that evening and found me on the floor asleep. I told her what had happened, and we cried together. She helped me get ready for bed. *Maybe tomorrow*, I thought. We can find out what that was all about. What I did know was that I could not return to work the next day, if ever again, because I was too afraid to leave the house.

*****

A few days later, Amber accompanied me to the psychologist's office. I was a nervous wreck. The apprehension of being attacked by anyone was foremost in my mind. Half walking and running, stopping and going, Amber convinced me it would be okay. When we arrived, I chose to sit against the wall so I would not have to look over my shoulder to see who was behind me. Speculative of everyone who walked in the office or came near me, we waited. Once in the office, I told the doctor what happened. He said he was hoping to avert my fears by sending me back to work quickly. Instead, it was too late; PTSD had set in.

"What is that?" I asked. He said it was Post-traumatic Stress Disorder, more commonly associated with the military from being in wars. He said that I had something in common with war veterans.

"What's that?" I asked. You sustained a gunshot wound to the head and lived to talk about it; however, most of them had not been so lucky. He said I had all my faculties and could take care of my physical self, but my mental state was in question. Strangely, I did not feel lucky. He said that he would report the incident to my employer to start the short-term disability process. He recommended that I go home and work with my insurance providers for psychological counseling.

On a dreary day in the middle of the week, I had several visitors come by. Serena and her brother surprised me, and as we were having a great time, my youngest brother Terell popped up. Terell was somewhat mysterious to me, as he wore tailor-made suits, carried a briefcase, and always had bodyguard-type guys with him. Sure enough, this was how he appeared on this day also, but more importantly, his visit was ominous. After the pleasantries, he turned serious and asked me for the names of the two guys responsible for the shooting. I asked him why he wanted to know, as my brother had a reputation for defending his sisters.

Once, when I was around seven, I was walking home with Vivian when some boys accosted us and took our candy. Another group of boys walked up and told the boys who my brother was. Not only did they give us back our candy, they emptied their pockets, gave us their money, then begged me not to tell my brother what they had done.

I learned at an early age that my brother had a "reputation," and some feared him. So naturally, when he asked for the names, I became wary.

I asked, "What are you gonna do?"

He said, "They gotta be handled."

"What does that mean?" I asked.

"They need to know they didn't just shoot any manager; you're my sister."

"Please don't kill them," I pleaded.

He said, "Okay, I just want them to know they fucked up."

Over time, the depths of my PTSD prevented me from being productive and temporarily did not allow me to care for my child. I wondered how I would continue to provide care for Alicia if the insurance ran out. She had been staying with her paternal grandmother since the incident. Her father had joined the military, and either his parents or uncle would bring her over to visit then take her back so that I could rest. This pattern lasted for several more weeks until I was able to care for her full-time. Alicia was the only bright light in my life. Thinking of her had saved my life. The thought of her encouraged me to get off the floor and call the police. Without my child, my life had little meaning. I had to get well so I could start caring for her daily as I was supposed to do. My daughter's love and innocence inspired me to call the insurance company and find a therapist.

My therapy appointments became my new ritual, as I went twice a week. I was given the Rorschach exam, a written multiple choice and a personality test. Strangely, the results came back with the finding that it was not the gunshot incident that brought me into counseling. Rather, it was the "straw that broke the camel's back." Evidently, I had been under so much pressure my entire life that I crumbled after being shot in the head.

Over the next few weeks of counseling, I felt capable enough to have my daughter brought home. I was then tasked with finding a daycare near our home. I made too much money for federally funded centers; however, I did not make enough money to pay full price at private institutions. I no longer wanted family members to care for her because it was time to prepare her for kindergarten, so I set out to find a learning center. As usual, there was Lance stepping in to tell me about openings at his daughter's school, which was our old private school. During the week, my new routine was to walk my child to school, come home, then find something constructive to do.

One morning I encountered a new shock. While walking down the hall to my apartment, a man stepped out, sliced my throat, and stepped back into the alcove where we put the garbage. I grabbed my neck as blood rushed through my fingers. I stumbled to open the door with my key, got in the house, and closed and locked the door. I ran into the bathroom and looked in the mirror. There was no blood. How could that be? I saw the man step out and slash my throat. I panicked and thought I was going crazy. My heart raced, and I started to shake all over with fear. I cried, screamed, and shouted, *Why!* I did not know this fear, and I did not know what to do.

When it was time to pick up my child, I walked down the hall and wondered if the man was still there. With trepidation, I walked close to the wall really fast and ran towards the elevator after I passed the alcove. Frantically, I pushed the button to go down. A hand stopped the door from closing. *Oh my God, he is going to get me! He is real!*

It was the landlord. I breathed a sigh of relief; he is not real. My daughter and I came home to a normal evening. My throat was slashed several more times as I walked to my apartment, and I became a nervous wreck. I did not know when the man would be there to assault me. He was never there when I was with someone, and no one ever saw him when I would ask them to go and check for him before I walked down the hall. I do not know if Amber or visitors thought I was making it all up, but they did give me strange looks. Years later, Amber told me she would tell our other sisters, who lived a few blocks away, to come check on me. She was disheartened when I told her they never did. At least I do not remember them doing so. My mind played a lot of tricks on me back then.

*****

By the fall of 1984, I was able to tend to my home needs and care for my daughter. I was still in therapy and taking medications to reduce the panic attacks and keep the headaches under control. Doctor Seymour Diamond, the headache specialist, advised that I would have headaches 20% of the time for the rest of my life. The medications reduced the panic attacks from me having multiple attacks daily to several during the week. However, nothing took away the new fears and intrusions that held my spirit hostage. I was cloaked with anxiety.

One day, while sitting on the couch, I got up to go to my bedroom and passed the mirror on the wall. There was one on each side. They were square sized mirrors with etched lines throughout. I had always liked mirrors as a teenager. My sisters and I would break them and put designs on the walls of our bedrooms. I had a big display of my boyfriend, Lance, saying I loved him, and my mother was not pleased. I carried my love of mirrors into my adult life. However, on this day, these mirrors deceived me. When I walked by, I saw a man's face. He appeared out of nowhere. He did not look like anyone I knew and was totally unfamiliar. I saw him when I walked by, turned around, looked back, and there he was! No smile or anger—nothing, just there. He was there every day from sunrise to sunset. In the middle of the night, when I woke up to go to the bathroom, I would check, and he would be there. When I came home, I checked, and he was there. Just there doing nothing, like a picture but human. He scared me.

While sitting on the couch one Saturday, I saw a panel of the wall near the floor move. I was stunned! *What is that?* I wondered. *Tick, tick*, just a little bit at a time, and it moved. There was paper spread on the floor, and I do not remember why. *Tick, tick, tick*. The crack got wider, little by little. Out popped a huge water bug! I hate water bugs with their big, black, hard shell of a body. I tried to kill one once as a child, and it would not die when I smacked it with my house shoe. I had to get a real shoe and whack it hard, then the shell cracked, and liquid oozed from its dead body. I have hated them since.

I quickly picked up my bare feet from the floor and curled them on the couch as I leaned over the side to see what the water bug would do next. The big, black bug struggled to turn over from its back. I was fascinated. Once the bug rolled himself over, it started jumping up and down on the paper, making this light clacking sound. I was entertained for what seemed like hours, and that was my fun for the day. My daughter was gone for the weekend. I had nothing to do and prayed for a visitor. I had cooked a lot of food, hoping to entice whoever visited with enough food for a long stay. No one showed up.

*****

On my twenty-fifth birthday, after being shot, I bought a couple six packs of sparkling wine and then went to Baskin-Robbins to buy a large chocolate ice cream cake. I was going to go visit my sisters. At the ice cream shop, I saw two young ladies I had worked with before the shooting and remembered that I did not treat them very well. While I could not remember why, I knew I owed them an apology for cursing them out. They were sitting in the back with some older women, maybe their mothers and other family members. I went to them and told them I was sorry for treating them so badly and apologized for not remembering exactly what it was I had done but told them I knew I had done something wrong. They all stared at me in bewilderment, and clumsily accepted my apology. I told them it was my first birthday, and I was going to celebrate with my sisters. I said goodbye and left the store.

I surprised my sisters with a visit and asked them to sing happy birthday to me. I insisted that it was my first birthday because it had been more than one year since being shot in the head, and God had given me a new life. It had only been four months. But they obliged and sang Happy Birthday to me; we drank wine, ate cake, and danced. I don't remember if I went home that night. All I know is I drank until I fell asleep.

The weekends would drag along sometimes. I rarely had visitors and my daughter was frequently away. My ex's mother had proven to be a loving grandmother who made sure my little girl was happy, and I was humbled by her attention. Over time, she became my godmother, as my mother now lived in Africa. During this period in my life, I needed advice from a mature woman, and our bond strengthened. I masked my mental illness. As far as everyone was concerned, I was fully recovered. I was in therapy discussing the issues and had everything under control. When someone did come around, I was the best hostess. When I did venture out, I brought something to drink or eat, and was the life of the party. I was upbeat, dressed well, and fun to be around. No one knew the dark corners of my life that held me captive between visits. Only Amber had some insight, but she didn't know everything.

There was a time when Amber came home from work and found me frozen in place, straddling the doorway. She freed my stiff hands from the doorway and led me to the bedroom. We sat on the bed, and as I began to tell her what happened, she covered her mouth and cried. For the first time, I shared my day with someone.

I told her I woke up that morning, and everything went as usual. The man was in the mirror on both sides of the wall. I had taken my daughter to school, stopped by the store, bought some groceries, and ran past the alcove in the hallway so the other man would not step out, slash my throat, and step back to his hiding place. I went about my day with housework, showered, and dressed to go out. When I unlocked and opened the door, I saw the man in the mirror's face change to an angry state, and it frightened me. But when I started to cross the doorway to the outside hallway, I thought, *Today will be the day I get my throat slashed for real.* So, I froze in stark raging fear. I was too afraid to go back into the house and terrified of what waited for me in the hallway. I had been standing there since about noon; it was now around 7 p.m. I was sticky from sweat, smelled from not being able to hold my bladder, and was stiff as a board. I sat on the side of the bed and cried profusely. I was falling apart and did not know what to do. Amber said she did not know what to do either. Then I realized I didn't know where Alicia was. I had dropped her off at school, but she was supposed to have been picked up hours ago.?

Fortunately, Lance had taken my daughter to his house. His daughter was two years older, attended the same school, and the girls played well together. He told me that when he saw my daughter was still at school alone, he figured I was detained, so he decided to bring her home. He said that he had rung the bell earlier in the day, and since no one answered, he took her to his home and waited until later to try again. I was thankful Alicia was okay. She had a good visit and seemed to like Lance. Seldom did I allow my daughter around any guys, but somehow, this seemed to work out with ease. Lance and I had talked on occasion since I had been injured. It was important to me that Alicia was able to be with other children to learn and play. I was grateful for Lance's attention and the care he provided for my child.

By that time in my life, my absence from work extended to long-term disability. I received enough money to care for my daughter's needs, and the rent and utilities were split in half with my sister. Though my mental capacity was a daily struggle, some things were normal, and I relished in the small stuff, such as someone caring enough to take care of my child without asking. Lance bringing her home in one piece with ice cream and smiles momentarily eased my fears.

My Love Returns to Me

SUNDAYS HAD BECOME THE designated day for laundry and hair combing. I would go to the laundromat across the street, start the wash cycle on a couple of machines, then come back home. On one particular Sunday, I prepared a dinner of barbeque beef short ribs, macaroni and cheese, greens, sweet potatoes, cornbread, and potato salad. My house was clean and I was finishing up the braids I put in Alicia's hair as I did every Sunday. The phone rang, and it was Lance. He wanted to know if I could wash and comb his daughter Patricia's hair. I asked him why his girlfriend could not do it; he said they had been arguing all day and did not want to ask her. I told him yes, on the condition that he would help me complete the laundry then stay for dinner. Once I told him what I had cooked, he agreed.

He came over a short time later, and while I did Patricia's hair, he went to the laundromat to finish my clothes. Afterwards, we ate dinner, and the girls played while he and I cleaned the kitchen. He asked me if I would watch Patricia so he could check in at home. I knew that meant to catch up with his girlfriend; that did not bother me. Sometime later, he returned with a perplexed look on his face. I asked him if he wanted to talk about it, and he timidly responded yes.

"Well, what's wrong?" I asked.

"I got into a big fight with my mother."

"About what?"

"She said that my girlfriend had been calling the house nonstop and that I needed to call her."

"Okay, what's the problem?"

"I told my mother I didn't want to talk to her anymore."

"Why not?"

"Well, that's what my mother asked too."

He then said what I did not think he would ever say to his mother. "I told her it's because I love Val!"

I gasped, "Really, you told your mother that?"

"Yes, I did."

"Well, how did your mother take that?"

"She said, 'That girl is not right for you, she's not good enough for you, and you should make things right with your girlfriend!'"

"Humph!"

No surprise there, I thought. His mother never approved of me because I was from the wrong side of the tracks. She and her husband were a part of the Black elite society of Chicago. He was a dentist, and she was a socialite. She did not think I belonged in her inner circle or her family.

"I told her that was too bad because I was staying with you if you would have me."

"You did it! You stood up to your mother for me?"

"Yes, Val. I love you and want to stay with you for as long as you will have me."

We hugged, then kissed, then put the girls to bed for the night. We stayed up and watched television and fell asleep on the couch, him spooning me. For the first time since the shooting, I felt safe. Our life began that day in the fall of September 1984. We spent every day together, and he eventually moved in. We got engaged several months later, in February 1985.

LIFE MOVES ON

AS WE EASED INTO the routine of taking care of our daughters, I started to calm down. I told Lance about some of my fears, and he listened. I do not think he understood, but I think he sensed something was not quite right. Since I never knew when I would be accosted by the knife-wielder in the hall, I could not say watch out or anything. Each time, I walked on his left when coming home and on his right when leaving. I made sure to look out of the corner of my eye for any signs of the knife-wielder.

All seemed normal until one night when Amber began screaming loudly. Lance and I jumped out of bed and ran to the front of the small apartment where Amber slept on a cot in the living room. We crossed over the short distance and I saw a man in a grey winter coat standing over Amber. He was staring at her, expressionless. The girls were now awake and had a look of terror in their eyes. I shook with fear. He had made it on the inside. The man of my many fears was real, and he stood over my sister as if in a trance.

The room had two windows near the cot, which both opened onto the rooftop. We had the windows nailed shut for security reasons. There was also a door on the opposite wall that had been painted shut and had a washer and dryer placed in front of it. So how did the man get in?

The painted door was open, and the washing machine was pushed awry. He was strong enough to push open a painted, locked door, move the washing machine, and get in. Lance grabbed a large, sharp knife and guided the confused looking man out of the house. Feeling nauseous, I went to the bathroom and noticed that the man had used the toilet and left blood and feces in the toilet. I flushed the toilet and felt sick to my stomach. Someone called the police, and we filed a report. We never saw the strange man again. The landlord later told us the intruder was the previous tenant who was mentally ill and still had a key. Instead of changing the lock, the landlord had just painted the door.

Over the next few days, I started feeling sick. My stomach was queasy, and I felt drained. After a couple of weeks, I went to the doctor and found out I was pregnant. This news, however, was not a shocker. Lance and I had already discussed having a child, and we figured since I was not working, now would be a good time. We realized it was time to move because our love nest was too small, and I no longer felt safe. Since Lance worked nights, he felt he had to do something to protect us in his absence, and I wholeheartedly agreed.

We found an apartment in a three-story multi-unit brownstone in the South Shore area of Chicago. We lived on a tree-lined street with single-family homes. The people kept up their property, and it seemed I lived amongst caring, hard-working people. I was somewhat reminded of the home in the suburbs I lived in with my mother when I was a teenager. The apartment had high ceilings, crown molding, hardwood floors, glass doorknobs, and large, airy rooms. Windows in the front welcomed the morning sun and cool breezes in the hot months, and the enclosed sunroom in the back served as an additional bedroom for my sister and a large bedroom the girls. There was a spacious, formal living and dining room, a large kitchen with windows, and a room in the basement for the washer and dryer. The five of us shared one large bathroom. A sigh of relief came over me. I felt safer in my new surroundings.

Becoming an instant family was a challenge, but I was up to the task. My days were spent tending to housework, a man who worked nights, two young girls, an unborn baby, and a live-in sister, as well as attending psychological counseling. And even though Patricia and Alicia went from being friends to sisters, it was not apparent at the time that Patricia resented having her mother replaced. The reality was that each of our daughters had a negligent parent they loved and possibly resented having a replacement.

Several months passed, and everything seemed to be going smoothly until the landlord knocked on the back door one evening. He told me that he had turned off the dryer, as it had been tumbling for several days. Embarrassed, I said thank you, and he suggested we get the timer fixed since dryers pull a lot of electricity and would increase his utility bill.

Lance asked me why I had not checked and turned off the dryer. I told him I was afraid to go to the laundry room because that man was waiting for me. Sometimes when I went down the stairs, he would lurk in the back by the garages or sometimes in the laundry room. I was trying to ignore him because he never wanted to talk to me, only look. He was not there all the time, but this last time, he frightened me, and I did not want to go back down after starting the timer on the dryer. A few days earlier I had tried to go downstairs, but he was outside the backdoor of our apartment; he had made it upstairs. When Lance asked me why I had not told him, I said that I did not want him to think I was still crazy. I thought when we moved, he would leave me alone, but he found out where I lived, and he was back. I told Lance I was sorry and was trying to be stronger and promised him that I would keep trying to be a good mother to our children and a good woman to him. I shamefully put my head down and cried. He held me and told me that it would be okay.

*****

As I settled into my new responsibilities, I realized I was bored. After taking the girls to school, I would come home, have breakfast with Lance when he came in from working the 3rd shift then go to sleep. I had nothing to do. Sometimes, I would walk down the street and become frightened of strangers or passing cars and rush back home. Besides walking the girls to their school, which was only a few blocks away, I did not venture far from home by myself, and when Lance woke up, the girls would be home. We would have dinner; the girls would do their homework, and he would go to work.

We visited family and friends regularly on his off days. One day while visiting his parents, I noticed an Atari gaming system in the living room. I asked my father-in-law if I could have it for the children, and he said yes. The gaming system was really for me, but I could not admit I had nothing productive to do during the day after completing my housework. Playing video games became my past time. After I came home from walking the girls to school and Lance went to sleep, I would start playing the games. My thumbs became numb, and I started getting small amounts of electric shock waves from the controller as the rubber had split open, but I kept playing and never complained. I did not realize I had become addicted to playing games until I started losing track of time during the day.

One day, I looked up and noticed that I was drenched with sweat and smelled musty. Startled, I quickly changed clothes, fixed myself up, and rushed out the door. I ran down the street to the school in time to pick up the girls. More time was lost as I fell into a depression. I stopped showering and getting dressed for the day, and the housework was ignored. After picking up the girls, my chores became bothersome, and I would rush to clean the kitchen, sweep the floors, and start cooking dinner. I struggled to make everything look normal so that when Lance woke up, the house would appear to be in order. Somehow, I managed to pull it off with little notice of my emotional unraveling. I had not told Lance about the man sitting on the garage roof outside the kitchen window. He was there at breakfast, during the day, and into the night.

Being a mother was starting to become a challenge. Both the girls were reacting to their new family structure differently. Attempting to raise two girls—one seeming to adjust to the sudden change in our family structure and the other showing signs of long-term problems due to her resentment— weighed heavily on me. One day while I was bathing, they asked if they could come into the bathroom to talk. They knew this was my private time and I did not like to be disturbed, but I let them in anyway. Once inside, they asked the most unusual question: The girls were curious as to who the baby would look like. Confused, I asked them what they were talking about.

"Who is the baby going to look like?" they asked again.

"He or she will look like daddy and me," I answered.

"No," they said. "Who is the baby going to 'look' like?"

I still did not understand the question.

They then asked, "Is the baby going to be light or dark-skinned?"

Was the baby going to look like my oldest or youngest daughter?

Not realizing the brevity of the question at the time, I simply said, "The baby will look like all of us because he or she will have a combination of my blood and daddy's blood." Later that day, I thought about what they must be going through as little girls who at one time played well together but were suddenly forced to be in a family with two people they barely knew. Lance and I had decided to be a family without considering how they felt. We made the decision based on how we felt about one another and assumed all would be well in our home. At the time, I did not realize how our decision to be a family would cause resentment and high anxiety for us all. Lance and I only knew that each of our daughters needed to be cared for by a mother and father together. I was the primary person at home and became burdened with a child who constantly misbehaved at school and started telling lies, which added to my stress during pregnancy.

Somewhere along the way, my girlfriends realized a baby shower had not been planned and started preparing a party. I was asked which of my sisters I was not in disagreement with and answered without knowing the reason for the question. On a Saturday afternoon, I was whisked away by a girlfriend and was surprised with a shower. To my amazement, Vivian was there finally meeting my girlfriends from the Muslim school, and a few of my sisters were also there. I had a wonderful time and was touched that someone thought enough of me to give me a party. Later, some of my sisters who were not at the party were pissed because they did not receive invites. I explained that I had nothing to do with it, but to no avail, it seemed to be my fault. When I asked the party planners, I was told that they did not want any stress around me for that day, so they decided to invite only non-combative family members. Indeed, there were many times when my sisters and I were fighting, but to me, it was natural.

While Lance was sleeping one morning, I was watching television when a commercial came on about uncontested divorces. Suddenly, I was angry with myself for getting pregnant by a married man and living in sin! With so much going on in my life, I had once again not used my head to think clearly in making adult decisions, and now I was within weeks of delivering our child. The advertisement said that an uncontested divorce was $475; that was the same amount as rent. I got up from the couch and went to wake Lance with my revelation. He was not pleased and was extremely irritated with my position. Somewhat hysterical, I told him how I felt about being pregnant by a married man and was not proud of myself for getting into this predicament. Confused, he asked me what should be done. I told him that I would pay the rent when due and that he should file for divorce from his estranged wife for the same amount of money. I demanded that he do it right then, and he was even more pissed. He angrily dressed, and I followed him out the door. He said that he did not need me to go with him, but I went anyway.

When we arrived at the attorney's office, I had to sit in the car because he was seething, having been awoken from his sleep and extremely tired from work. When he came out hours later, he showed me the draft document, and we headed home. I felt somewhat relieved; however, us getting married was not discussed. Several weeks went by, and after haggling with his estranged wife over some minor details, she signed the papers. The divorce was finalized shortly thereafter, and Lance said he was ready to marry me. I wanted to wait until after the baby was born so that I could have a proper wedding, but he insisted on doing it then.

On November 15, 1985, an uninteresting and drizzling morning, Lance and I drove our daughters to school, then went downtown and got married. Lance and I said "I do" in the Judge's chambers at City Hall in Chicago nine days before our son was born. Five things about this day stand out in my memory: it was a cloudy day, the judge had badly stained teeth, I did not feel pretty, and sadly, Patricia cried when we told her the news. Lance later told me that she did not understand why we had to get married. When he told her that he loved me, and we were going to have a baby, he said she still did not see why we had to get married. He said that even though we all lived together, and I was having a baby, she thought one day, the two of them would move back in with her Nanny and Papa. She was seven years old, and he never had a talk with her about us being a family. The final thing I remember is that I got into my first fight with Serena because she had planned a surprise for the day, which fell through when I changed the plan for the day without telling her. The result was no lasting memorabilia for my wedding day because Lance did not want me to tell anyone.

The arrival of our baby boy was met with love and relief. Giving birth to my son was as beautiful as deciding to be a mother to my first child. Though equally painful as my daughter's birth, in the end, the wonderment of becoming a mother is one of joy and happiness. We went home two days later, and our new life began. Life moved along, and I had a new purpose. Determined to be successful with a new baby and a growing family, I forged ahead in bliss. Learning to manage my days was met with new energy, and all seemed right in my little world. We had outings, visited family, and had picnics, and the strange man was no longer ruling every day, just some of them. Patricia still struggled to find her way and her place in the family, and she cried for the mother who lived far away. There was a time when she acted out so badly in school that I spanked her before going to and coming in from school because she was in trouble almost every day. I had gotten to the point of running out of ideas to encourage good behavior. I rewarded her with treats of her liking when she did well. I saw that she liked to dress herself, so I allowed her to pick some of her own clothes. She started combing her hair and caring for her personal needs at an early age. However, my stresses may have interfered with her individuality, as I often dressed the girls like twins, which could have attributed to her not finding her place in the family. Yet, I wholeheartedly did my best in caring for her.

Parent-teacher meetings had become a regular occurrence, and I was frustrated. Sadly, one evening after being spanked while kneeling on the floor and crying, she put her hands in the praying position and tearfully said, "Mommy, come and get me please." I was shocked and hurt when I realized she was not crying for me; she was pleading for her biological mother. I felt sadness, mortification, and then I was besieged with humility. I stopped the punishment, helped her off the floor, and took her to her bedroom. I went in the bathroom, wet a towel, went back to the room, and washed her face. I then gently asked her if she wanted her mother, and she said yes. I hugged her and apologized for whipping her.

Later that night, after I put the girls to bed, I called her mother and explained the situation. I told her that I did not know how much her daughter loved her, whether it was 90% or 10%, but either way, I could not tap into that part of her because it was reserved for her. She asked me what she was supposed to do, and I told her she needed to call her daughter the next day and start connecting with her. She went on to tell me that she had sent her daughter to live with her father because she thought that he could provide better than she. I sternly repeated what I thought she must do and she agreed to call her daughter the next day before she went to bed.

The following evening after homework and dinner, Patricia received a phone call from her mother, and she excitedly relayed that her mother promised to call more frequently. This little girl had the biggest smile on her face;

however, her mother was not good at keeping her word. As time went by, I would have to call and insist that she stay in contact with her daughter. It seemed to be an effort in futility, yet I thought it was the least I could do for the child. Her behavior did not improve much, and my naivety did not help the situation. Lance told me that I had opened a can of worms.

As time passed, my relationship with Patricia's biological mother swelled into regular conflicts, which only served as a power struggle between two women for one child. At the time, I believed my way was best since as I was the daily caretaker, and it appeared her mother seemingly struggled for her place in our family. The battle between the two moms caused much anguish for Patricia, who suffered the most, as any child would.

Regardless of how much I had on my plate with my family and mental challenges, I always managed to present myself as a well-balanced individual who had it all together. I was still haunted by the strange man who made me fearful of what he might do to my son. It seemed that some days when all was quiet, I could not shake his presence. He seemed to always lurk in the background, waiting to pounce. I struggled to make sense of my life. At times, I was happy with bliss, and other times, I was depressed with worry. Fearful of taking my son out for walks coupled with hurrying from walking the girls to school, I lived in a state of panic. Sometimes, the man would be in the vestibule when I opened the door of the building or sitting in the stairway on the way to our apartment. Other times, he would pop up out of nowhere and raise the hair on the back of my neck. I took my prescriptions for headaches, depression, and anxiety. I continued my bi-weekly appointments with my psychologist.

Lance picked me up one day from the therapist's office and told me we were going to New York for the weekend. He had planned for the kids' care and said we could buy what we needed when we arrived. Excitedly, we went to the airport and left for the weekend excursion. We had a fabulous time visiting with his brother and two sisters. The food was wonderful, walking down Broadway was magnificent, and the trip was perfect. I was refreshed with renewed spirits when we got back home to Chicago.

Hard Parenting Lessons

Occasionally, I had snacks for the girls when they came home; however, Patricia's appetite began to increase, and she started asking for more food. After several days, I asked her if she was getting enough lunch at school, and she said no. When I asked her why she said that she did not have money for lunch. *Impossible*! *We give you money every day*. She then told me that a girl in her class was taking her money. Immediately, I knew I had to fix the problem without making my child look like a snitch. So, I asked my daughter if she was scared and if she liked the girl. She admitted some fear, but mostly, she did not know why the girl had decided to pick on her. I assured her that I would work something out and fed her more food.

The next day, while the kids were on the playground, I went up to the school and spoke with the teacher. I told her what was going on and asked her if I could contact the other girl's mother to invite her to a family outing. Maybe if the girls got to know one another away from school, the other girl would ease up on my child. The teacher thought that was a good plan and worked out the communication. The following weekend, we went by the girl's house to pick her up. We went roller skating and had a pizza lunch at Giordano's in Hyde Park. We took the child home, and I hoped the two girls had bonded enough to make my child's school week less frustrating. When Patricia came home on Monday, I asked her about her day at school with the girl. She reported that the girl said that she liked our family and had fun. She said if she could come out with us again, that would be cool. More important to me was that the girl said she would leave my daughter alone. However, my child said she did not want the girl to come with us anymore because she did not like her enough. Patricia stated the girl was not her friend.

In another instance, as if to battle with good versus evil, Patricia repeatedly mentioned another little girl in her class that had even worse behavior. Her name was Penny, and she was a nightmare of a child; she cursed, talked back to teachers, and was constantly fighting. I told Patricia I did not like her befriending her, but she seemed to be attracted like flies to shit. One afternoon, I went to the school to pick up Alicia and decided to check in on Patricia. I could'nt find her.

I went to her teacher and asked where she might be, and together, we searched. To no avail, she was not found on the playground where she was supposed to be. I asked the teacher if she was with Penny, and the teacher did not know a girl by that name. I explained it was a child in her classroom, and the teacher, in a perplexed state, said that she did not have a student by that name. I insisted she show me her attendance book, and once I realized the truth, I panicked. *Where was my child?* Hastily, I walked quickly out of the school with Alicia, who was pushing Lance Jr. in the stroller, trying to catch up with me. I was running up to kids and turning them around, and became anxious when I realized none of them were Patricia.

A student finally told the teacher that Patricia had left campus with another group of kids. Finally, Patricia ran up behind me, and when I asked her where she had been, she pointed to where she had been playing. I went into total "black mamma mode" and snatched her little ass up by the collar and took her home.

After losing my mind with all the yelling and screaming about the things that could have happened to her in the streets, she finally admitted to me that Penny was her imaginary friend. She had made up this bad ass little girl who was really herself, and when she was constantly telling me Penny's "antics," she was, in fact, telling on herself. I was relieved to know she had a conscience but saddened to realize the depths of her troubles. Lance and I attempted counseling, but after a few short weeks, we stopped going since the therapist stated that she would not talk. I did not have the mental capacity to think of an alternate plan. I let it go.

Though Patricia exhibited behaviors that caused me to constantly think of ways to teach and guide her in the right direction, I could not escape the harshness of my realities. I was unskilled in being a stepmother. To me the enigma was the unknown factors of her being. More specifically, I clearly understood Alicia because I knew her father and his family; unfortunately, I did not have an intimate knowledge of Patricia's mother's family background. For me these things were important because a child's psychosis could be inherited, or just possibly circumstantial. Being that I knew firsthand how it felt not to have a mother, hell both parents, present during my young formative years, imagining how Patricia felt having an absent parent was too disturbing to consider. I did not know the answer to this question, and she was at that tender age of possibly, not knowing how to ask the question of, *Why isn't my mother here?* These were the problems during the "honeymoon" period of our marriage in which neither Lance nor I could address the dire questions with realistic answers to put us on a healthy path.

To be honest, I didn't know how to have a constructive conversation about the troubles I was having with our oldest child. The knowledge and guidance a healthier family would get from their elders did not exist for us. Neither Lance nor I had a support system in our parents, and we did not have support from siblings who could offer us advice as to how to adjust and/ or build on our family structure. We were, in essence, the first family on both sides to marry and become step-parents, although his parents too were step-parents, they did not offer us words of wisdom when I asked for help. We instead attempted to be what most people saw us as: a successful unit built on a long-lasting friendship, bounded in love since 1973. Without vocal or mental support, I endeavored to build my family just as I did anything else: by myself. I would persevere and fight through it.

*****

At some point in my life, I realized how unequipped I was mentally; yet I didn't realize that my inability to handle some daily tasks ran parallel with a disability.

At the onset of leaving work and being placed on short-term disability through my employers, I had to also apply for social security disability.

Each application was denied, and every six months, the insurance company directed me to reapply. As the process moved along, I started to receive a long-term disability check each month. This process continued for about two years until one morning the phone rang while I was washing dishes. I answered the phone with a whisper,

"Hello."

"May I speak to Valorita Gill?"

"Speaking," in my whispered voice.

"Hello, did you say this was Valorita Gill?"

"Yes."

"Ma'am, why are you whispering?"

"So he can't hear me."

"So who can't hear you?" she asked.

"The man."

"What man?"

"The man on the roof."

"What man on the roof?"

"The man who sits on the roof outside my kitchen window."

"Why does this man sit on the roof outside your window?"

"I don't know. He just sits there watching me."

"How long has he been sitting there?"

"I don't know; maybe a few months."

"Well, ma'am, can I call you Val?"

"Yes, sure." I continued to whisper.

"Val, do you have another phone in the house?"

"Yes, there's one in the living room."

"Okay, Val, put the phone down and go in the living room and take the phone off the hook. Can you do that?"

"Yes, I think so, but I have to be quiet, so he doesn't hear me."

I put the phone down in the kitchen, went into the living room, and picked up the phone. She then asked me how I felt. I spoke in my normal voice and told her I was much better. The caller told me that she was calling to assess my situation, as I had applied for disability based on a mental disorder. She asked me a series of questions about how I spent my time, and I told her everything. I told her about the man who wanted to slash my throat, the man in the mirror, the panic attacks, the one in the laundry room, and the one on the roof. I also told her about the home invasion and the police report and that I played Atari all day to manage my day. She went on to say that she had recently completed a class on how to deal with PTSD and that she would approve my disability request. She apologized for what I was experiencing and for the agency taking so long to validate my condition. She said to expect the final determination in the mail along with a phone call. I was approved for Social Security Disability in a letter stating I was permanently disabled due to a severe mental condition. I called and asked them what that meant and was told that I was permanently disabled. I asked for more clarity and was told that I was unfit to be employed and that my disability would eventually be replaced with retirement at age sixty-two. That made me sad.

Being classified as a mentally disabled person did not sit well with me. Even though I had a man tormenting me for the past two years, I had hoped for recovery. I had built a protection of sorts around me in the event of being attacked by a stranger, and my trust level was low. I did not think about working. Instead, I concentrated on being a good mother to my children and took care of my home.

VERIFIABLY UNFIT

ON JANUARY 1, 1987, we needed a change. Our daughters were growing up fast, and I began to fear they would have bad experiences similar to mine. We wanted out of the city and yearned for something different. Fortunately, Lance was looking for a career change, and in his pursuit of happiness in his professional life, we looked to move south, as he inquired about work from friends who had already left Chicago. My sister Amber had moved to Atlanta to be married. Her husband had started sending along job openings and one of his friends had started looking for an open position within his company. Lance was interviewed for a position with a reputable engineering company as a Network Engineer in Huntsville, Alabama. He was offered the position with a start date in February 1987.

Over the next two weeks, I was busy with closing the apartment for the move south. I did not allow myself any time to think about what was to happen next. Lance and I collected boxes. He rented a truck for moving and made plans to turn off the utilities. I retrieved the girls' school records and got the vaccination cards from the doctor's office so that school enrollment would be effortless. I had packed up the apartment and was cleaning up when I suddenly had to stop. I sat down on a chair, looked around the living room, and realized I had not prepared myself emotionally for the change.

When I told my sisters and Clay that we were moving, they did not take me seriously. I had called Serena and informed her of our sudden decision to move, and she was stunned. She had wanted to throw a big going away party but wasn't expecting us to leave so soon. My response for leaving earlier than originally stated came across as callous and uncaring. My tone set us on a new course as we had never really disagreed until then. Unfortunately, it would be several months before we discussed this matter, and I realized I hurt her feelings.

I went downstairs a few days later and picked up the mail to be rewarded with a card from Vivian. She wrote to me and told me how she just realized I could no longer come to her home for a visit and that we would no longer be just a bus ride away from one another. She told me she realized our friendship would undergo a new test and that she did not want to lose me along the way. I stared at the card and cried because I realized I was leaving everything I knew. Then the doorbell rang. Another girlfriend dropped by to tell me how sad she was that I was leaving. We shared a bottle of wine, and after catching up with one another, she left.

I planned to go to the Baton Club in Chicago with my girlfriends during my last weekend Chicago. The Baton was a new female impersonator's club and we had a blast. Our favorite impersonator was a Diana Ross character, but the entire troupe of actors were stunning experts. Even though I had one friend send a heartfelt card and another come over, and I was going out with a group of friends, I had not heard from any of my sisters. Not one of them reached out to say anything of value to me. I felt instant loneliness because I thought my family would plan something for me before we moved away. I was saddened because none of them seemed to care. "Oh well," I thought. I guess I am on my own. I still thought I was close with my sisters, but apparently, I was wrong. Things would be different from here on out.

My relationship with my sisters was challenging, at best. Seemingly, our discourse widened as we aged, but it was more like the devil had interrupted our lives, and our disagreements became mean and somewhat hateful. I know I had started a different life after marriage and my mental state caused me to be less patient with bullshit. Nevertheless, I thought we had enough in common to keep us together. Unfortunately, it was the glaring differences that tore us apart. Though I was not the first to marry, I was accused of sitting on a high horse. Maybe that was true, as my mother once told me that I would either become a judge or Mother Theresa. Neither profession seemed right for me, but from Mother's position, I was too judgmental yet caring at the same time. An oxymoron of sorts, I thought, but undoubtedly true. I did expect people to behave differently and work within the law. And yes, I was very concerned about the wellbeing of others and helped out whenever possible. However, I did not think these characteristics would be turn-offs to others; certainly not my sisters.

Although our struggles and lives were different, I often disagreed with at least one sister every few months. I do not know if it was me becoming more difficult and less tolerant or if we were growing apart. Either way, the fights became a strain on what I thought was a close relationship. As my time in Chicago shortened, my excitement for the move finally arrived. I gathered the kids, closed the apartment, and turned in the keys to the landlord. My distant cousin Virgil drove the kids and me, while Lance and a driver traveled separately with our belongings.

The long car ride to our new home was exciting and arduous at the same time. Seeing the landscape change from the large city and the four-lane highway going from I-65N to I-65S was startling for a person who had basically never traveled beyond the city of Chicago. In the winter of 1987, the natural process of the leaves falling off the trees and black dirt covered with snow had already taken place. The sky was dreary, and it was cold outside. As we got closer to the south, the landscape started changing. Crossing the Ohio Bridge from Indianapolis to Louisville gave one last glance at big city living.

As we rode deeper into the south, crossing the Mason Dixie line, I thought about the racial tensions black people endured before civil rights. I had put little thought into the changing of cultures and how it would affect my young family and me. It never occurred to me that change was coming in a form totally unfamiliar to me and that I was ill-prepared to handle life's new twists and challenges. Instead, I marveled at the color of the dirt changing from black to red clay.

I remembered a childhood friend from when I was around six or seven years old, who would come home from being down south and tell us about eating red dirt pies. We only pretended to eat our black dirt pies filled with small pieces of glass, but she said that she ate hers because it was different from what we had up here. I do not know if I believed her, but right then, I remembered this vividly as I marveled at the sun shining hotly on the bright red dirt. The large vacant fields also were different. In Chicago, when you saw a vacant lot, it was because someone had bulldozed an abandoned building. Yet, this vacant land was undeveloped property. I was curious if anything was ever on the land, or if it was only for farming. Years later, these fields would be covered with wind tunnels reaching towards the sky with whirring sounds as they rotated, creating renewable energy.

Several stops and many hours later, we finally exited the highway. In the stark darkness with little light to guide us, we continued the route to our new home. A few miles from the highway, we spotted our turn into the first apartment complex I would ever live in. It was advertised as a luxury complex resplendent with two pools, one with a hot tub, multiple tennis courts, playgrounds, an exercise room, and a clubhouse. The living area and kitchen were small but the bedrooms were large. The master had its own private bath and a walk-in closet, while the girls shared a nice sized bedroom, and Lance Jr. had his own room. There was a closet in the hall for the washer and dryer, a fireplace in the living room, and a small patio.

The complex was relatively new, and not only was it different, it was also pretty. There were plenty of trees and winter foliage, and the smell of wood burning in the fireplaces set the mood as homey and friendly. I liked my surroundings, and it appeared we had made a good choice to start our new life here. As with most new moves, the first night is cumbersome with settling children, figuring out the first meal, and knowing when to stop and start up the following day. Our journey had just begun, and I anticipated a smooth transition irrespective of not knowing anyone outside of my little family.

The next morning, we set out to register the girls in school, and thankfully, I had done my homework. The kids got into school without any problems. Next, we took a tour of our new city, and I realized it was the complete opposite of Chicago. The contrast was astounding, and I was pleased with my decision to move forward in life as opposed to staying in one place to fight under abnormal conditions. I was in a world quite different from the one I was in a few years prior when I lived in an abandoned building. Driving west on Highway 20 welcomed a booming, growing city with the standard fare of restaurants, gas stations, banks, K-Mart, Food World, Winn Dixie, and the engineering companies Intergraph, Teledyne Brown, and Wyle Laboratories. The road heading south on Wall Triana opened to the industrial park where the Chrysler and Kholer plants were located, along with medical malls, airport transportation offices, Huntsville/Madison International Airport, and the Boeing company— our reason for relocation. The campus was impressive, yet we could not visit because Lance had not checked in, and the facilities were closed to the public. By the time we finished exploring our new surroundings and having lunch, it was time for the girls to come home on the bus. They each said their day was okay and lamented about the dialect of the south.

A few weeks later, when I heard Patricia joking about the southern dialect, though at the time funny, I stopped and reminded them that articulation of words was important and told them not to make fun of differences in people. I realized I might have a bit of a challenge assimilating to the new surroundings and the mindset of my adult peers. Surprisingly, my acclimatization to the suburban housewife's daily routine was quite simple. I learned to present myself as other wives in my community did, including drinking wine poolside in the afternoon and the evenings after the children were put down for the night. I started drinking to fill the void of loneliness. Drinking became a past-time.

There is a saying in the south: there are only two seasons, summer and winter. This is because, in April, the weather changes from a low 40° to 80° by May. With a hot sun, low winds, humidity, and a heat index of another +10°, pool time is in mid-May. The routine for housewives was to get the kids to the bus, go home, clean the house and the toddler(s), and be at the pool by 11 a.m. We would bring snacks, magazines, water, suntan lotion, toys for the children, and chill poolside. Around 2:45 p.m., we would all go home and get ready to pick up the children from the bus stop, get them in their swimsuits, and go back to the pool. At 5 p.m. we would go home and start our evening activities, which included cooking dinner, helping our kids with homework, and waiting for our husbands to come home.

At this point in my life, I felt like a "Stepford Wife." I did not socialize with the other women beyond our daily activities. At the time, I had not found comfort with being around culturally and ethnically different women; I missed my friends and sisters back home. My adjustment to the culture of the south would take more than ten years. Until then, I worked towards improving myself and attempted to fit in with my new surroundings. The struggle was real, and the challenges I encountered slowly became a focal point in my daily life. Unfortunately, I did not realize my struggles were our struggles, and everyone had a degree of "getting used" to the new environment.

Later in life, I was bewildered with the awareness that my problems were the driving force of my everyday activities and failed to realize that my husband and daughters were also affected by the decision to move south, away from what we all knew. It is amazing how the psyche works, when a person is having a problem, a bigger problem is taking note of how what you are going through affects others and that it is not always about you. My mother had always told me that no man is an island and that any decision you make affects everyone around you. I was still a student in Mother's classroom and did not know it.

*****

Fortunately for Lance, he built a social life with colleagues. Since I did not have much of a social life, I devoted my attention to Lance Jr. I realized that at three years old, he needed the exposure of being around other children his own age. We agreed to put him in daycare from 9 a.m. to 12 p.m., and I decided to go back to school. I enrolled at the University of Alabama in Huntsville, aka UAH, and took two English courses. I passed with a B in each. School was escapism, but after those classes, I could not figure out what to do next, so I continued to concentrate on my family and tried to stay busy until I figured out what I wanted to do with my life.

Considering Lance was building his career and traveled a lot, I became the disciplinarian to Patricia in his absence. This became a sore spot between us because, by the time Lance came home from business trips, I would tell him about Patricia's behavior and he wouldn't believe me. His disbelief was shocking to me because I thought he should know I would not lie. His disbelief made me feel he did not trust me to care for his daughter and treat her fairly.

The reality was that Patricia was in constant trouble, and maturity brought more drama into the household. The parent-teacher meetings were regular, the punishments ceaseless, and the arguments between us—*exhausting*. Lance's return home each time was welcoming and disturbing, as she and I had our own versions of what happened in his absence. Lance failed to learn how to judiciously settle matters as the head of the house. Patricia's biological mother would call the house and his work to bitch about how her daughter was treated by his wife, and he straddled the fence instead of addressing any situation. His inability to play an active role in the upbringing of his child became a wedge in our marriage down the road.

In the meantime, learning how to parent and love a child who held deep resentment was my reality. I struggled to be a "better" mother to my children than my mother was to me. I only knew what I learned in Mother's house and had yet to find more constructive ways to discipline my children. My mother had favorites, and her punishments were not always fair. In my opinion, love and support did not seem to exist in her home. In time, I eventually found my way, but at that time, my children were subjected to learned behavior.

To me, the difference between the girls was that Alicia hardly ever needed discipline, participated in activities, and made excellent grades, while Patricia showed keen interest in socializing, stayed in some type of trouble, and made mediocre grades. To me it seemed pretty obvious where the problems lie, so I found it ridiculous for anyone not to see the differences. More importantly, I struggled with not constantly comparing the behaviors of the two girls. My fear was not finding a way to balance the two dissimilar behaviors without showing favoritism. I did not want to prefer one child over another because I genuinely loved Patricia and wanted the best for her. What was most difficult was the reality that the kids were not getting a fully functioning mother and Lance didn't have a have-it-all-together wife. Instead, what they had was a woman who was desperately trying to prove that she was mentally and physically capable of rearing her children, being a good mother, and a loving, supportive wife. I was failing miserably and did not know how to ask for help. In the meantime, I continued to do better with the hopes of one day learning how to love, support, counsel, and become a mother to both daughters without fear of failure.

As my frustrations grew from household matters and my husband's travels, I decided to enroll in a community college to earn an Associate's Degree in Business. Going back to school was exciting as it allowed me time to thrive amongst like-minded people while building on my future of one day, possibly working outside the home again. My new schedule was to see my husband off to work, get the girls to the bus, and my son to daycare. I came home, straightened the house, went to school, and in the evenings, we had family time. School was three days a week, and to stay active, I joined the Student Government Association and the Newsletter team.

Sadly, the strange man had found my new address, and he was visiting me again. I first noticed him one day while walking back home from the bus stop. He was near the dumpster where we put the garbage for pickup. He was hiding from me, and when I first saw him, he stooped down low so I could not see him. At first, I thought my eyes were playing tricks on me, but I was too scared to go and search. Over the next several days, though, the man let his presence be known by waiting until I had a full view of him before he stooped down then looked back up. He clearly saw the fright in my eyes, and I saw the mischievous smile. I ran up the stairs and fumbled with my keys to unlock the door. Once inside, I fumbled with the lock to secure the apartment. My heart raced, and I wondered how he found me and what he wanted with me. My nightmare had started all over again, and I did not know how I was going to get through this one because I was now living in a safer environment far away from the dangers of Chicago. I thought it best not to tell anyone. I went back to taking life one day at a time and hiding my problems from Lance.

The mean-faced man became a constant in daily life again, as he also showed up at school. He would camp out in the lobby or the doorway exiting the building, and he would be outside my home when I arrived. He showed up on the playground when I took my son out on weekends, but I never saw him around the pool, nor did I see him when we went on family outings. He only came around when I was alone or with my son, heightening my fear of him harming Lance Jr. As frightful as my life had become, I continued to do my housework, parent my children, go to school, and do my best to provide for my family. While taking a nap one day, I tried to open my eyes, and in my blurred vision, I saw a man standing over my bed. I could not tell who he was or what he had been doing; I just knew that I had a hard time waking from sleep. The man looked unfamiliar, and he was not a Black man. In fact, this man was White in a maintenance uniform, and I wondered if he worked for the apartment complex. Not sure of who he was, I tried hard to wake up, but to no avail; I went back to sleep.

When I woke up, I remembered the man and my struggle to wake up from sleep, but nothing else was different. I had no signs of being violated and wondered if I had been drugged. I searched my arm for needle marks because whatever that was felt so real. Again, no evidence of anything out of the ordinary, so I just pushed the memory out of my mind and concluded it was a dream. More importantly was for me to succeed daily and not show weakness because, to me, the other side of weakness is fear and then failure. I could not afford to fail. I had to be good at something since I was a failure towards myself. If I did a good job with my family, it would look like I was doing well for myself, thereby appearing to be successful. Until I could ratio-nalize why I was haunted by these men, I chose to move forward in hopes of one day having answers.

Something New

SEVERAL YEARS LATER, WE moved into a rental property. It was our way of learning how to care for a house before purchase. Even though our life in the south was in full swing, what I missed most was family and friends. Then out of the blue, we received news that my sister Jasmine needed assistance coming back from Ghana, West Africa. The country was going through a civil war, and she, her husband, and three children were displaced. They needed someone in the states to say they could come to stay with them, and we excitedly accepted. I was overjoyed with having a sister to visit for a while and anxiously awaited their arrival.

After completing work with the State Department and proving we could indeed house them, Jasmine was given flight information and was able to call me from the US Embassy in Ghana. I had not spoken with her since she was fifteen, when Mother moved overseas with her and Beryl. We had written a few letters and exchanged pictures over the years. She was now around twenty-three, with a husband and family. Having someone here who loved me and who I could talk to would be a good thing. The day her flight came into the Huntsville International Airport, I packed up the kids, drove the short distance, and parked the car. They were hours late because her husband caused them to miss their flight while on a stopover in New York. Nevertheless, her plane finally arrived, and I anxiously awaited seeing my sister.

When Jasmine came down the aisle, I cried with a sigh of relief. I was amazed at her sun-kissed brown skin and golden flaked hair. Her beautiful bright smile and colorful headdress reminded me of the movie *The Color Purple*. With children in tow, I ran to her. I hugged and kissed my little sister, then grabbed her baby from her arms. Her girls looked at me and told their mother that I looked like Safta, which means grandmother in Hebrew. I met her husband David and we all walked through the small airport to the baggage area. David idled along as he took the time to look at the posters and roamed the gift shop.

I finally had an adult female to talk with in my home. Though I had met some women and considered a few of them friends, nothing replaced a sister. We talked for hours and shared our adult lives. She said that her neighborhood in Monrovia, Liberia was bombed when the war started, and for several days, she and her family were trapped and surrounded by rubble in her home. She spoke of her hunger and the long walk they had to endure before arriving in another city and finding refuge. Somewhere in her story, she told me how she and her family had moved on to Ghana, West Africa. I was thankful she had survived her ordeal and resettled somewhere safer.

Her life had become even more of a struggle, and she wanted to come home. She reached out to the US Embassy since she and her husband were American citizens, and the US government made provisions to send the entire family home. I felt proud of my country and its ability to care for its citizens around the globe.

Jasmine marveled at modern technology and stated how long it had been since she had cooked on a stove or washed dishes in a sink. I shuddered to think of how she must have been living prior to coming to my home. For as happy as she was to be in our home, she needed time to acclimate to her surroundings. Her previous homes were in undeveloped regions of Africa. She was now face to face with stark cultural differences. Though for a short period we lived in a predominantly White community, Jasmine was now unfamiliar with life with White people. She thought Black people in America had become somewhat strange, although they were more familiar than White people. The differences between White and Black, West Africa and America, were stark. She said it would take a while before she got used to her new surroundings.

Over the next few days, I went about my routine of going to school and taking care of the children and home. A few weeks later, my sister Sapphire sent her two children down for a scheduled summer vacation. My house was full of love and kids for the first time in a long time, and I welcomed every bit of it. We had two men, two women, five girls, and three boys under one roof. That translated into a lot more mouths to feed. Jasmine and her family were vegans, meaning the grocery bill more than doubled since we had to purchase more fresh fruits and vegetables and less processed items. She pleased us with a vegan meal one evening, and it was tasty. That is when I saw the first mean streak of her husband.

After Jasmine served David his food, he came over to the stove and started slamming pots and covers around, pissed because he could not have more food, even after he had two helpings. I looked at him as if he had lost his damn mind, and Jasmine looked at me with an expression of *"Please don't say anything."*

His nerve! I thought. I later told Lance, and he seemed to shove it off as if it was okay. A day or so later, Patricia and Alicia came upstairs and complained that Uncle David had been watching television for several days from morning to night, and it prevented them from playing Nintendo. I asked him about that, and he said he was fascinated with television, so I responded, "Put your fascination on a schedule so that the children can watch the television also."

So far, I did not care too much for this man. The last straw was when Jasmine came upstairs after Lance left for work and began crying. David had slapped her in the face. I got up and proceeded to put my clothes on. She asked me what I was doing, and I responded, "I'm going downstairs to kick his ass for slapping you." She asked me not to and said that she was only telling me what happened but didn't want me to do anything. I told her that Lance was not going to be happy when he found out, and she asked me not to tell. I told her I would because he needed to know he had an abusive man in his home. I told Lance, and he had a talk with his brother-in-law. He thought that would suffice, but I was not satisfied. I wanted revenge, and it came sooner than I could have planned.

Apparently, David felt the need to show his appreciation for living off us, so he decided to cut the grass in the back. He treated the task as simple because it was hotter in Africa and he did not nourish himself as he pushed the gas-driven mower up and down the backyard, which was an acre of land. By the time I came home from school and work, he was ill with what we thought was a cold. Unfortunately, it turned out to be malaria. He maintained a high temperature, was in severe pain, but did not trust going to the emergency room. He suffered for several days, and I did little to help after my sister told me that Quinine would relieve him of his pain and cure him quickly.

However, several weeks later, Jasmine, also broke out with a bout of malaria, and I panicked. Seeing her writhing in pain and sweating profusely, I set out to help. I called around to the local pharmacies looking for Quinine and got lucky with a location near the hospital. They said they only kept a few, as this was not a common illness in the area. Under the circumstances, they decided to sell them to me. David asked if he could ride with me, and I said sure. We went to pick up the medicine and came home. On the way back, he asked me why I did not get any medicine for him. I told him that I did not like him, and it was my understanding that he would be okay. He told me that was mean. I said, "Yes, but so are you every day to my sister, so suffer and try not to get sick again."

In addition to helping Jasmine get used to her new surroundings, I continued to keep it together by focusing on work and school. Jasmine decided to keep the house in order in my absence and cook dinner as well as look after the kids. Then, one day, Amber called from Atlanta and said she and her family were driving up to visit. Happy times came quickly, as Jasmine and Amber were only a year apart and had a closer relationship. Their homecoming was bittersweet, and they seemed to hug and cry for a long period. I was elated to have two sisters in my home at one time. Lance came home, and family time was a shared experience for all, except David. He seemed to be annoyed with our closeness and questioned our sincerity since neither of us had visited them in Africa. His statement seemed ignorant, so I asked him how much he thought it costs to visit Africa. Though this man was originally from New York and walked away from a full academic scholarship to attain his master's degree, he lacked common sense. He stated that since we were doing so well, he did not think money was an obstacle.

Seemingly, some people think America is the land of milk and honey and materials things are easy to acquire. They don't realize we must work hard to achieve success. What they think is a lot is actually very minimal. Unfortunately, the next day Jasmine called me at work in a panic, stating that David wanted to know if they could go back to Atlanta with Amber to relocate. I told her that did not make much sense and questioned why they wanted to move suddenly. She said he did not like the way I was treating him and wanted to move. I hung up, called Amber at her hotel, and we agreed to have a family meeting that evening.

Later that day, after Lance came home, the three couples sat down for a family discussion. Basically, the out-of-touch brother-in-law wanted to move on to where he thought he would get more help than what we were providing. Amber and her husband told him that he was in the best place possible if he was looking to get support. We all attempted to work out a plan because we knew the struggle ahead would be cumbersome, and David's imagined support team would be more than likely nonexistent. It did not matter; he was determined to leave with my sister and their three little kids. His arrogance was stifling, as if he wanted us to beg him to stay and for me to promise to treat him better. None of that happened. Amber and her family left to go back to Atlanta, and I went to work the following morning. While at work the next day, Jasmine called me around noon to tell me a cab was on the way, and it would take them to the Greyhound bus station in Huntsville for the ride to Atlanta. We tearfully said our goodbyes over the phone, and she left. After about six months of moving from house to house with people he knew, they went back to Africa.

BACK TO WORK

OVER THE NEXT TWO years, the only thing that seemed to change was my completion of Junior College with a degree in Computer Operations. The journey took longer than I had originally planned because I had to change my major from business. I talked to one of the educators who told me that I would not be successful in business in the south because I was too light to be Black and too dark to be White. She did not think White society would accept me into their business culture. I assumed that since she was an authority figure, a brown-skinned black woman, highly educated, and a native of the south, she knew what she was talking about. I changed my major with ease, with the thought of anything dealing with computers in 1992 was sure to pay off in corporate America.

Learning more about computers also provided insight into what my husband did at work. Often, I would ask him about his day, and his answers would fly over my head, leaving me clueless about how to respond. Sadly, I saw the same teacher walking down the street in her slip, house shoes, and a mink coat in the heat of the summer months. Someone later told me that she had a nervous breakdown. They said it was unsurprising because her mental health had caused her to slip in and out of work. I remember feeling frustrated because she had convinced me to change my major from a field of study I believed was right for me; I later graduated with honors and celebrated with Lance and the kids.

Good times were short-lived as I tried to find a job with my degree, only to discover that without experience, I was not an ideal candidate. I settled on a job working in fast food again. I applied for an Assistant Manager's position with a restaurant in Madison and was invited to an interview. During the interview, I was asked why I had left the workforce for several years, so I explained my health condition. He asked why I wanted to work since I was receiving disability, and I responded, "I believe I can make more money." He hired me, assigned me to a store, and gave me a start date and several uniforms. I left the office excited and anxious to get back to work, but the thought of going back scared me.

Out of nowhere, I became weary and anticipated danger; I shook with fear. I sat on the bed and started to sweat as my heartbeat accelerated! My head started hurting, and my hands felt clammy and sticky. With shaking nervous hands, I picked up the phone and called the hiring manager to tell him I could not do it and hung up before he questioned me. I was embarrassed and felt defeated for not being able to go to work. I felt disgusted with the realization that I would have to receive disability benefits instead of working outside the home.

Several weeks passed, and I awoke one day with a new spirit! I was happy to be alive, thankful for my life, and ready to move on. It felt like God was giving me another chance to be successful, and I seized the day! I felt stronger and fearless as I called the area manager and apologized for not showing up to work. I explained my panic attack and conveyed how desperately I wanted to contribute to society by working for him. I assured him he would not be disappointed and told him how diligent an employee I would be. I convinced him that he would benefit greatly from having someone with my go-to attitude and willingness to make his store more successful. He laughed and gave me another chance. He said that he respected me for wanting to try again and for not settling for what life was throwing at me. I had a new report date and showed up thirty minutes early, eager to start again.

I went back to what I knew and hoped for the best while praying to overcome my fears. I started with showing my proficiency in the basics of mopping floors, wiping down counters and cabinets, and cleaning the lobby and bathrooms. I moved on, learning how to cook fries during and after the lunch rush. I was taught how to cook on the grill. I learned how to make desserts, fill drinks, and make ice cream. I was a fast learner and proved to myself that I could do this work with ease. Quality products and excellent customer service are trademarks of any business, and success comes from efficient, dedicated employees.

I was back in the world of employment and felt somewhat satisfied as an individual. Employment catapulted me into the atmosphere of working with unfamiliar cultures. This became my first learning experience in diversity, and the lessons were quick and hard. After I settled into my new employment, I called the Social Security Administration and informed them I was employed and no longer needed the disability check. I was asked the type of work I selected and was given an appointment for an evaluation. After I met with a psychotherapist, I later received a letter from the social security office informing me that I still fit the definition of a mentally disabled person, so my children and I would continue to receive monthly checks. I continued to work and completed the bi-annual assessments by a medical professional, praying one day, I would cease to qualify for disability.

Though I enjoyed my new work environment, the attention to communication was a challenge. Madison/Huntsville is a diverse living area because of the many government contracts. The employment here invites the educated to come to the area to thrive and become successful in their endeavors, attaining a piece of the American dream. Due to the quality of life that North Alabama offers, families are successful and can afford their children comfortable lives. Young adults and teenagers in these families benefit and thrive due to their parent's success. In most cases, they are afforded cars at age sixteen so that they can drive to school and work. The living conditions also foster an atmosphere of entitlement and privilege that I was not accustomed to.

I came from a poor welfare community, and kids walked or rode the bus to school and work. Some kids worked to help out at home, while others, like me, could not find a job or were unable to work. The kids in this area had life handed to them, and most of the ones I worked with wanted to make something of themselves because their parents' success inspired them. My discomfort was with a few of the adults who appeared to have little desire to want more out of life. Most troubling was their resentment towards me since I was hired into management, never having worked in a burger restaurant.

It was as if they could not grasp the concept of prior fast food management experience.

It seemed I was being set up to fail as an Assistant Manager. Money would disappear from my cash drawers during the day, and the routine of setting up food stations and stocking the front counter with items needed for the oncoming shift was not performed. As my frustration grew, I was startled when a male assistant manager visited me one evening to let me know how troubled he was regarding some of my coworkers' attitudes towards me. Apparently, some of the women were sabotaging me in an attempt to get me fired. This was eye-opening and explained the missing money and low front counter stock upon my start of shift. Grown women were acting like teenage girls. Do not get me wrong, coming from the southside of Chicago instilled grit and toughness in me. Street fighting and defending myself was in my blood, but there was one adjective that sent me to a negative place, and I carried a chip on my shoulder for it. He told me that they referred to me as a high-yellow heifer. In black culture, that is a no-no; those are words that start fights. The term is derogatory and implies one is too light to be Black and too dark to be White, thereby assuming some mongrel status to look down on.

Being called high-yellow also carried with it the stigma of slave times when light-skinned blacks were treated better (house Negroes) than other slaves. The term also opens the door to assume some in black culture thought themselves better than those with more melanin because they could assimilate into White society. In fact, I have never heard of a complimentary way of referring to light-skinned black people. Since my family has differing hues and had never once considered skin tone an issue, I took offense at being disrespected amongst my peers, especially in the workplace. Hence, I felt that I had to defend myself.

Infuriated, I spoke with my store manager and asked him to intervene because I did not want to engage in the neck popping, finger-snapping, loud, angry black woman's response these ignorant women obviously deserved. The manager was from the south and was young; he chose not to get involved. He said he could not do it and was afraid to get between angry black women. As time went by, my disappointment with my job became more apparent, and I started to feel uneasy about my team. One day prior to shift change, I was in the freezer performing an inventory, and the door suddenly closed. I calmly stopped counting and went to open the door, and it would not open. Trying not to lose my cool, I knocked on the door for someone to open it. Minutes passed, and no one came. I started to unravel and banged on the door. When it finally opened, I went to the manager and told them why I could not be in the freezer with the door shut ever again. I had to leave work immediately to keep from exploding, as I felt nauseous, and my head started to spin. I realized this was someone's sick idea of a practical joke. I further realized God had not brought me this far to settle for nonsense. While contemplating my exit, I came to work one evening and heard the restaurant next door had been robbed at gunpoint. The police visited the store later in the week and stated the criminals had picked up the floor safe and took it out of the store. The burglaries had started down the street and were working their way up to the corner. They anticipated that our establishment would be hit within the next few days.

I quit on the spot.

Realizing I could no longer use my only skillset to find employment, I sought to find a new career path. I adjusted my resume to reflect my associate degree in Computer Operations, management experience, office work, and the ability to work with others. I emphasized my attention to detail and ambition. I scoured the area, hoping, anticipating, and praying something would stick; I came up with nothing. I believed the reward for my education would be a good-paying job. As such, Lance and I worked towards creating a future rich with some material possessions and a good living.

The struggle to find work was real, and I became distraught as I continuously failed in the job search. One day, I answered an ad in the newspaper for an office clerk position at an engineering company. I interviewed and was hired, pending a background check and the passing of a drug test. Assured those were easy to achieve, Lance took me shopping for a business wardrobe. I started work and was proud of my efforts to secure a position in corporate America. No longer would I have to be concerned with being robbed, working with money, backstabbing co-workers, and long work shifts. I had a straight Monday through Friday shift from 8 a.m. to 5 p.m. I was no longer trapped working in an environment that pressured me to adjust my thought process because of the imminent fear of being robbed at gunpoint or shot after compliance. Real or imagined, those were my fears every day while working in the fast food industry. I now had a real chance at being normal while at work. I seized the opportunity to be a good employee and make the company feel they had made the best decision by taking a chance on someone who had little experience working in an office. I had ninety days to earn a permanent position, and I intended to soar with ease over the next several months.

Transitioning from fast-food to working in office administration happened with ease. Dressing professionally instead of wearing a uniform was refreshing. Learning new work was invigorating, and meeting new people inspired me daily. The ninety-day trial period seemed to go by quickly and I looked forward to the offer of a permanent position. When I started to work in the office, the filing seemed impossible, with folders stacked high on each cabinet and scattered around the office. I quickly implemented a filing system and efficiently filed everything away while processing new orders for delivery to other key personnel whom I supported.

After several weeks of nonstop work, it all slowed down. I thought it strange and became curious about the sudden lack of work. I went over to the high tower where work originated to check out my concerns. I took the elevator to the 6th floor, where the engineer admins worked and blatantly inquired if any of them had noticed the slowing of work. As heads popped up over the stacks of folders, I knew immediately I had asked the wrong question. The glaring looks that followed told me to exit quickly and not come back. It was then I realized the admins had a system of working by always appearing busy, and unbeknownst to me, I had essentially stepped into a hornet's nest. I gave the appearance of efficiency by consistently completing my work at the end of each day while it appeared that they carried work over for job security. Still, I did not see it coming. I was terminated on the 89th day of work. I was told that I was not a good fit and was escorted out like a thief. I walked with my belongings in a box with my head low to my chest. I endured the humiliation of separation from employment in my first corporate position, but I also felt encouraged. I would learn the tricks of the trade and how to get along with office personnel. I needed to figure out how to shine without dulling someone else's light and how to become successful in a career of my choosing. I set out to become a temporary worker.

I refreshed my memory on the numerous career seminars I had attended while in school, which gave advice on how to assimilate in office environments and how to be an efficient, reliable, and dependable employee. However, nothing taught me how to be less aggressive in the south; talk less, listen more. I quickly learned that just because you think it does not mean it needs to be said. These were the little things that carried a lot of weight. I had to learn the hard way and take some prisoners along the way, including my brash self.

I also brushed up on my typing speed and went to the library to research careers. I scoured the indexes for information on which careers paid well as opposed to those that did not and the qualifications needed for landing employment. I researched resume writing and how to list reliable references, as these were important aspects of finding a job and developing skill sets.

When I felt I had enough in my arsenal to become a temporary worker, I contacted various offices in town and requested to be on their roster of employees until I could find a permanent position. I was tested for basic typing and filing and was accepted onto a team. As a team member, I was afforded training on a variety of office software applications so that I could qualify for open positions across town. After a couple of weeks, I was sent out on my first job. The job was a basic front-office position that included answering telephones, scheduling appointments, typing memos, and maintaining a face in the front office. The work was easy, boring, and the beginning of many positions to follow, some for weeks, others for a day. Every position mattered, and I learned a little something everywhere I went. I worked in offices for companies that provided construction, bookbinding, fabricating fireplaces, and engineering. I treated each assignment as an opportunity to become a full-time employee and patiently waited while learning all I could. In the meantime, I worked during the mornings and was at home to care for my family in the evenings.

Over the next several years, I registered with five agencies and made enough money to substantiate my thirst to work. I worked with one agency long enough to earn a week's paid vacation, while at another, I was selected as employee of the month. Though not a permanent worker at any company, I received some employee benefits across various agencies. My salary varied from $5.25 to $8 an hour, and I started to resist positions that paid less than

$7.50 an hour. While watching a talk show, I heard about a wonderful book by Dale Carnegie entitled *How to Win Friends and Influence People.* I made the purchase and immediately started reading this book. I was reading the chapter "How to Land the Job" when I got a call from one of my agencies stating there was a position as a temporary to permanent admin at a major engineering company. I was ready!

Preparation for the interview was exciting because I had my number one supporter, husband, and friend, Lance. We went shopping and selected a navy, fitted suit made of raw silk with a beige blouse, beige stockings, and navy pumps. I went to get that job and had never felt more confident about anything in my adult life. At the end of the interview, I asked the manager if he had any more people to interview, and he said yes. I told him it was not necessary because he was looking at his next admin. I left the facility on top of the world and then realized I had put inaccurate information in my resume. I called my agency to explain, and before I could state the reason for the call, I was told that the Lockheed Martin Human Resources department from the interviewing company had called and said to cancel all other appointments because the position was mine. The jubilation I felt, the tears of joy, the excitement in my chest culminated into a feeling of overwhelming accomplishment. I had succeeded in attaining a position in corporate America with a company that was respected worldwide. I felt I had achieved the impossible. I knew I would become a full-time employee over time, and they would make me one of their valued employees.

ARE THE CHILDREN NORMAL?

MY CAREER WAS WELL on its way and home life was improving. Lance Jr. had learned to use the power of persuasion with the ladies at a young age. One day at the pool, I was talking to an attractive female in a bikini. We were standing and drinking something frothy when Lance Jr. walked up and stared at the woman. His eyes started at the top of her face, and he slowly glanced down her body. As he looked down, stopping near her waist and hips, he continued his mischievous journey to her feet. She looked at me as she covered herself with one arm across her body and said, "Why do I feel naked?"

I responded, "Because he just undressed you with his eyes."

On another occasion, I picked him up from daycare, and his teacher pulled me to the side and said quite frankly, "I saw him hit that boy and push that girl and could not punish him." I asked why not, and she said, "I just love him, and if I could freeze myself and wait until he was twenty-one, I would." I told her she should have whacked him on the behind. She said, "No, I could not reprimand him because he is too precious." Before I said anything else, she informed me that she had requested removal from his class. Okay, problem solved; this type of favoritism was not acceptable.

Realizing this little boy's ability to manipulate women, I had to warn his teacher on his first day of school in kindergarten. I was asked, "Is there anything special you need to tell me about your child?" I told her to watch out for his eyes because he had a way of getting out of trouble with them.

She told me that was ridiculous. *Okay.* It was not long before she sent a note home asking for my attendance on a matter of concern.

Once I arrived in her class, she said, "That eye thing your son does, how long has that been going on?"

I told her for about a year and asked, "Why, what is the problem?" She then said that she had never had a little boy that could use his eyes to get what he wanted. He had gotten into trouble, and she struggled with reprimanding him. She agreed that she should have taken my advice seriously. We worked on a path forward to support each other from then on.

Communicating with all my children's educators proved to be the best way to stay on top of important matters. Working on the punishments together was paramount to making my children understand that I worked with their educators and we were a team. Lance Jr. once got in trouble in the fourth grade for cursing. The teacher, in this case, sent home a letter. After I spoke with my son, he told me he cursed the boy because the boy called him a *nigger*. Remembering the power of words, I found it necessary to write a letter to my son's teacher explaining why he had cursed. In the letter, I used the newly coined phrase the "N-word" to describe the derogatory term used against my son. I thought that I was communicating in an adult manner with another adult-minded individual. Unfortunately, the next day, I was perturbed by her response. The teacher had the audacity to write another letter to clarify why "Little Johnny" was offended because my son had called him a "Motherfucker" and that was why he was called a "Nigger." She had the unmitigated gall to spell out each word. Seething with fury at her inability to see what was wrong with this picture, I wrote another letter using my mother's tone:

> *"Dear Ms. So-and-so,*
>
> *While you may think it appropriate for "Little Johnny" to call my son the "N-word," just so you know, there is never an appropriate time for a black child to be called anything outside of his or her name, let alone being called a Nigger. And since it is obviously okay with you to use the term so freely, you must also feel the same way. So, I am going to do you a favor. When my son comes home today from school, I am going to ask him how*

his day went. He had better tell me that he learned a lesson about tolerance and the importance of treating all people with kindness. He had also better tell me how nice you were when you apologized for not correcting the matter with Little Johnny in a timely manner and that you are sorry for hurting his feelings by not treating him like he was as important as the other kids in the classroom.

Now, if my son says anything opposite of this, I will report you to the principal, school board, and the local news stations as someone who tolerates name-calling and disrespect in her classroom and that you have little tolerance for minorities."

Although the next day Lance Jr. did give a good report as I had hoped, his teacher sent yet another note stating that he stuck his tongue out at her and that it hurt her feelings. I replied with another note advising her to find another job because obviously, she was not a good fit for working with children. I used this opportunity to teach my child the importance of respecting everyone, especially his educators.

Lance Jr. did not get into much more trouble throughout his schooling; however, he did become the class clown for a short period. He pulled the fire alarm on the third day of his fifth grade, and while I knew better than to fall for his affection, I must admit, it worked. I knew I lost that battle. I later walked past his bedroom and saw him standing up to a picture of me on the wall, kissing and rubbing my face saying, "I love you, mommy, so much." I melted, and it would be years before I could stand up to anything that he did wrong.

Our youngest daughter Alicia appeared to do the best in school. When she missed the bus one day, and the principal offered to take her home, she refused because he did not know the code word. The principal called the house, and I told him what it was; he repeated it to her then stated how impressed he was with that security tip since saying code words in the late '80s was new to society. She continued to be a low-key child until I received a call a few years later in middle school that she had walked out of the classroom.

Once I spoke to her, she told me that she could not go to the bathroom between classes because the lines were too long, and she did not want to be tardy. However, when she asked the teacher on several occasions, she was denied. She said she had to either walk out or pee on herself. I spoke with the principal and asked him what she should have done? I stated that I did not think she should be reprimanded, but he said something had to be done because he did not want other children to think they could do the same. We agreed on a mild punishment to keep the rules in place. When she came home from school, I explained why she was being punished and the importance of rules. I also explained that sometimes being tardy for the right reasons was better than being late for the wrong ones.

There was a time when I got my first credit card and purchased everyone a gift, wrapped them, then gave them to each person. The girls got pajamas, Lance Jr. got a toy, and hubby got a bottle of cologne. By the weekend, I heard the washing machine going and went to check it out because I typically was the only one who did the laundry. To my surprise, there were only two items in the washer, and they belonged to Alicia. I asked her why she only washed two items, and she said that I had always told them to read instructions and follow directions and the label on the clothes said, "Wash separately." She said she did not want to ruin her new pajamas because they were so pretty. I turned my head and laughed. I learned then this child would take everything at face value. In middle school, she joined the band, which is when volunteering became part of my routine.

*****

Patricia never quite settled into the family. I struggled with her daily, and I became frustrated and told her father it was too much since it took away from the other children. Lance did not believe Patricia lied, talked back, and treated me with little respect. I threw my hands up and told him, "I quit." He had no choice but to become her primary caregiver until she completed the ninth grade and moved out west. As her primary caregiver, Lance took her to track practices, and I no longer was involved in anything dealing with her school or social activities.

After a few weeks of a seemingly blissful arrangement, Patricia's ill-behaved antics became evident, and Lance was livid. It had snowed one day, and they made plans for him to pick her up from school. He walked in the front door of our home and wondered where she was since she was not at school. Patricia walked in a few minutes later, and he asked how she had gotten home. She responded that she had ran the three miles. Incredulously, he asked her again, and she stuck to her lie. Lance then told her to go outside and run back to school to prove it as he followed her in the car. With delight, I watched her start the run while he drove.

He returned home minutes later with her in the car. She could not run to the corner with her backpack and converse sneakers in the snow. It was not because she was tired; running with sneakers on in the snow with a backpack was nearly impossible for her. She admitted her boyfriend dropped her off. Since she was only fourteen, she was not allowed to be alone with a boy. Lance learned that the things I had been saying about Patricia had merit. Lance continued as her primary caregiver, which eventually caused our relationship to weaken. Life in my home became toxic.

After school let out for the summer, Alicia's father sent for her, and I left for Chicago to stay with my in-laws. This was my attempt to show my husband how life would be without me while at the same time allowing him and his two biological children to have bonding moments. I hated leaving my son; however, I knew my departure was for the best. I didn't feel wanted or appreciated, considering his ex-wife's meddling and her mother's bullshit had become a part of my life. When either of them called, Patricia made them believe she was being treated unfairly and punished harshly for her bad behavior. To make matters worse, Lance failed to stand up for me as I needed him to as the head of the house. Patricia eventually asked her father if she could live with her mother instead. Unbeknownst to me, they had a quiet arrangement where all she had to do was ask, and he would oblige the request of her moving to California to be with her mother. I welcomed the move because I was tired of all the antics. After Patricia completed freshman year, Lance put her on a plane, and she moved to Los Angeles to be with her mother. Finally, I was able to concentrate on the two children who had been ignored over the years.

FREEDOM

As TIME WENT BY, I became a full-time employee at work, and I was happy. Lance and I were both employees of two powerful companies with international reputations. I regularly volunteered at the kids' school and with their afterschool activities and recreational sports. I put my whole into supporting my children so that hopefully, they would never feel the void I felt as a child regarding my mother. I also flourished at work and started establishing new relationships with women of all ethnicities. To my surprise, the black women I worked with were secure and successful and accepted me into their circle. In fact, one day, I noticed how comfortable I felt and took the time to visit each one (there were only about ten of us). I thanked them for not treating me unfairly or disrespecting me because of my lighter complexion.

I looked at my career as a place to grow and become a part of its fabric. Around December 1997, I saw a flyer promoting the startup for the Diversity Leadership Council, and I decided to attend. The company had a representative come in and discuss the layout and corporate vision. I volunteered to help set up the council and was selected as the Chairperson. Excitedly, I worked with other employees to make our facility one of inclusion and coexistence. I learned firsthand the importance of tolerance and acceptance of people with differences and how diversity is not only about skin color; it includes culture, geography, family, religion, society, and a myriad of other differences amongst all people. I grew as a person and was empowered to make friends with women I had shied away from at the beginning of my move South, who were White. I learned we had more in common than our differences, and this attitude allowed me to grow inwardly. I later volunteered for all organizations within our facility—professional and social. By the end of my first year of employment, I had been selected as Employee of the Year and received the Director's Award. Over my tenure, I received numerous awards for professional accomplishments and volunteerism.

With new girlfriends from work, Black and White, I started socializing after work. I had maintained a relationship with a good friend from my first job in fast food. I had not been clubbing since I was a young mother and I started going out with her every other weekend. That did not last, though, because I could not appreciate the meat market atmosphere, and after about six weeks, I was done with the single girl club as a married woman. I decided to go out with Lance if I wanted a club scene. However, we really could not get into the nightlife much since The Cotton Club, Nimbus, Chick Rick's, and Ding Bats in Chicago were our examples of fun nightlife. These smaller joints in Huntsville did not impress us. Also, when I went out, the awkward stares and snarly treatment from brown-skinned sisters were disturbing. Since I was still uncomfortable in my own skin, mistreatment heightened my uneasiness in public places with the sisters.

One time I went out with a girlfriend to a New Year's weekend concert. When we went to the restroom, the sisters got quiet and had the *"who the hell is she"* facial expression. Exhausted, I said to her, "When are black women gonna stop looking at me like I'm not one of them?" She responded, "I don't know, girl; it's just that way down here." Sometime later, in another situation at a sorority/fraternity function, after dancing for what seemed like thirty minutes, the floor emptied, and we all rushed to the facilities to freshen up. Again, when I walked into the restroom, I got the stares. This time I flipped the script and decided to embrace my skin and hair. I took off my jacket with much flare and said, "Damn, it's hot!" Then I started shaking my head up and down, moving my hair in the breeze I created. In exaggerated motions, I started wiping the sweat from my brow and said loudly, "Y'all hot, too, right?" My friends looked at me and said, "Girl, you crazy!" It was then and there, at almost forty years old, I learned to be happy with the skin I was born in.

*****

We purchased our first home when Alicia was in high school and Lance Jr. was in Middle school. While Lance and I were in our twelfth year of marriage, he was still traveling a lot, but it did not bother me as much. I now had friends and the kids were growing up fast. I had discovered freedom and traveled to Chicago regularly. On every trip home, I connected with Serena. By then, Vivian had disappeared, and I patiently waited for her to show up. I visited with my sisters also, but we were different. I always came home feeling depressed and tried to grow into a better person when I returned. I hoped that one day my sisters and I would reconnect and have happy times again. I never did much when I went back to Chicago. It was mostly visiting family and going out to dinner with Serena. The time went by fast and then I came back home. Other times, we went as a family, and the routine was not much different, other than a visit to the in-laws. The in-laws were not welcoming of me, so I did not put much effort into getting in their space. I did visit Alicia's side of the family, as I still enjoyed being around my godmother. Time always went by fast, and I did my best to avoid drama with my sisters.

*****

On Thursdays I took Alicia to band practice, and on Fridays, I volunteered during football games. When hubby was home, we shared the chores around the house and went out for dinner with the kids. However, it seemed we were drifting apart, and we hit a dry spell. We were well beyond the seven-year itch, but I could not put my finger on the issue. Maybe my work had exposed me to new freedoms, and I had started to depend less on Lance, or maybe it was because he was gone so much and I had learned to make it without him.

Whatever it was, I was worried because I knew my love for him was forever. I also knew I had changed. I was no longer haunted by the strange man. He disappeared without me noticing. It seemed the more confident and independent I became, the less I noticed him. I never learned why he was there or why he left. More importantly, though, he was gone. Still, I had held on to my protection of always checking the doors at night and double-checking the alarm before I went to bed. The windows stayed locked, and my inner sense remained keenly alert to danger. I no longer suffered from panic attacks, but I still had troubling headaches. I admit there were times when I looked over my shoulders, and some things made me uncomfortable; however, I was greatly improved and enjoyed my life. My life was finally settling into something that made me feel proud. Then an abrupt change halted everything.

One day, while having a stress-free day at work, I got a call from Africa informing me that my mother had a serious illness. Stunned, I called my siblings and told them we needed to work together and get mother home immediately. Remarkably, Mother was home within two weeks. We agreed that I would accommodate her, so she traveled to the states and then to our home. Shortly after her arrival, my siblings descended on my home as we all worried about her health. Mother had quadruple bypass heart surgery a couple of days later. For most of my siblings, this was their first visit to my home, and someone initiated a family meeting regarding unsettled business.

The drama quickly unfolded as one sister tearfully told her story of being abandoned by us after marrying her second husband. Though quite sad, I decided the timing was not good. I resented them for wanting to work out problems that originated in Chicago in my home. Since this was, unfortunately, their first trip South, I did not want the visit to turn sour. I wanted happy times during this unfortunate gathering. Mother's surgery was fresh in our minds, and I preferred not to have negative distractions. We instead switched topics and found ways to be peaceful and make the best of a horrible situation. Two weeks after her surgery, Mother came home, and Diamond stayed behind to help.

Time slowly came and went, and Mother was recuperating. While watching television two weeks into my mother's recovery, Lance called me into the bedroom. Annoyed by the disruption because I was enjoying a movie with my mother and sister, I went to the room and saw Lance rolling across the bed in pain, mumbling that he had a headache. I sat on the floor and watched him squeeze his head as his eyes bulged outward in pain. I had experienced excruciating headaches in my past but never had I witnessed someone with such discomfort. I asked him if I should dial 911, and he said yes.

We arrived at the hospital's ER, where a neurosurgeon was able to tell us what was wrong. Lance had an AVM (arteriovenous malformation), a rare condition that very few people are born with, and few have an intrusion. An AVM is a defect in a person's vascular system that can interfere with the natural flow of blood from the heart to the brain. The doctors said they knew almost everything about the human heart, but the brain was an enigma. Having been in the hospital's ER two weeks earlier for Mother's heart attack, and now facing my husband's health scare, I was mentally and emotionally overwhelmed. As I stood with Alicia in the hall, waiting for instructions, I silently cried and prayed for God's mercy.

Lance was admitted into the Neurological Intensive Care Unit (NICU) for observation for a few days, then was transferred to a private room. I called Lance's parents to inform them of their son's illness and was told by his father I did not know what I was talking about. Insulted, I hung up the phone and proceeded to make more phone calls. Sometime later, his brother Arthur and their mother came down for a visit. His mother traveled back home that same day. That evening I received a call from Lance's father apologizing because he learned from his wife that Lance had indeed suffered, as I explained. I was told that I had proven to them that I obviously loved their son because I didn't leave him during his weakest time. I felt alone with my teenage children, even though I had my sister Diamond and Arthur for support.

After about a week and a half, Lance was released from the hospital. I spoon-fed him, and I assisted him with personal functions until he was stronger. For a period, there were two recovering patients in my home, and since Diamond was able to ride back home with Arthur, I was alone with teenagers whom I had not prepared for medical emergencies. They had been sheltered from hardship and not been exposed to struggle, and I felt that I had failed by not teaching them about sacrifice. I did not want them to experience hardships and now could not fathom change for them. Instead, I took on all duties until Lance went back to work.

After six months of living in my home, I could no longer deal with my mother's presence. She left to live with Ruby in Milwaukee but not before she and I attempted to shout out our differences and reconcile our relationship. I eventually told her it would be best if she just answered a few questions I had about my childhood, and I would be okay. I informed her I would be easier to talk to than my sisters, who were waiting for her with their unresolved issues. Mother attempted to answer the basic questions as to why she abandoned me and, of course, she did not think she had abandoned any of her children. I told her how I felt about learning how to brutally fight my sisters and how tiresome it was caring for her children when I was just a child. She could not provide me with enough information to make me feel better. I asked her why she seemed unattached to my well-being and still Mother had no answers. However, she did say she loved me and just did the best she could with what she had to work with. I asked her what that meant but she did not have a response. I decided to let it go.

I felt empty and less invigorated to move forward with the prospect of a better relationship. Truthfully, I felt duped. I resigned myself to believe Mother had nothing else to say regarding this matter. We eventually managed to come to a resolution we could both move forward from, and I was mildly okay. I realized there was only so much I could do since so much time had passed and ownership for her failings as a mother at the time was not easy for her. Selfishly, I made sure Mother was gone before Mother's Day, as I did not want to share my day with her. I did love my mother; however, I had not forgiven her for not being there for me when I needed her in my younger years.

*****

As time rolled around, life went back to our normal, as Alicia prepared for her high school prom and graduation. This was exciting for me since I had little fanfare for mine and did all that I could to make hers memorable. I lived vicariously through her and enjoyed these two experiences. For her graduation, we sent for, Patricia, and invited her father and his family, my mother-in-law, and her godmother Serena to celebrate the momentous occasion. I cried when she walked across the stage to receive her Honor's Degree and she had earned a full band scholarship to attend Alabama A&M University. I felt as though I had struggled with every bit of me to care for my daughter and the payoff was worth the tireless, sleepless struggle of my life's breath. Witnessing her accomplishment filled my heart with pride, and tears of joy trailed down my face. Her graduation was marked as another one of the happiest days of my life.

In the fall of her graduating year, Alicia started her collegiate education. Around this time in my life, I had been promoted to a technical position, working more closely with the engineers. While spending time in the computer lab, I noticed I could not relate to some topics and felt inadequate during conversations. I decided to go back to school to earn my bachelor's degree. I wanted to accomplish this goal before Lance Jr. graduated from high school; he was fourteen years old then. I wanted to converse intelligently with my coworkers, and I wanted to lead by example for my children, to show them the importance of education. My employer's paid tuition for college, so I enrolled and started online courses with the University of Phoenix in Information Systems. Online schooling proved challenging as every five weeks, I completed a class and selected another one. My husband and I were still seemingly growing apart, but we kept it moving since we realized we were devoted friends, and loyalties did not diminish, yet there was an emptiness we both were feeling. Our marriage was in a rough patch, but we decided to persevere and take it one day at a time. It seemed that the passion had gone on a long vacation and forgot to tell us when it was coming back home.

Gotta Trust God

One day, I received an e-mail from Jade reporting that Pearl, who had been struggling with drug addiction, had given birth to another child. Prior to Pearl's drug addiction, she had only smoked weed; however, she had been in an altercation involving cocaine and was set on fire and left for dead in a motel room. She started using street drugs—crack cocaine—and, fortunately, had birthed several children without drugs in her system at the time of their birth. She had her older children before her addiction, but the next six children's lives were in greater peril because, by then, her addiction had taken control of her life. Pearl was living a precarious life on the streets with little contact with family members. I constantly wondered how she was doing and how she was surviving. As time went on, no news was good news as she continued to birth children. Someone always made a way for the children one way or the other. None of them were in the care of the state as all of her children were provided for within the family and grew up close, and sadly, each had a story. Hearing the news that she had another child, and he was born drug-free, was welcomed news to our family since the child born three years before had been born with drugs in his system and had been taken from her at birth.

A few weeks later, Lance and I talked about our marriage. We agreed that we were in unchartered territory without direction to make it better. I told him that while we figured things out, I was going to Chicago to meet my newest nephew, Marion.

By the time I arrived in Chicago that November 2000, it had just stopped snowing. I was ill-prepared for the now unfamiliar winter months. This was my first trip in the winter without Lance, and I was weary and anxious to settle down for the night. After I retrieved my car rental and arrived at Jade's home I became frustrated because no one was there. Plan B, I went to visit my godmother until my sister returned home. Always happy to see me, she let me in, and we enjoyed a long visit. Several hours later, Jade and I connected, and I went to her home to settle in for the night. Excitedly, I went up the stairs and was greeted by Jade, who was bewildered and ruffled by the day's activities. Sitting on the chair, I encountered my first experience with someone on drugs. Pearl was in a drug-induced state, mumbling and nodding in and out of sleep. She had an unfamiliar smell that was akin to funk, sweat, and uncleanliness. As Jade was describing what happened, I kept looking back at Pearl wondering if she could hear us talking about her.

The story was that Pearl left the house the day before with her baby and did not return. Jade was worried since she did not know where Pearl was. Pearl's oldest son called and said that someone known for selling drugs had come over and wanted to leave an infant, Marion, with him. Unaware of what to do, he told the person to keep the baby.

In her fury, Jade rushed to our nephew's home, picked him up, and went to find the baby. As they drove around the neighborhood looking for anyone who might know his mother, they saw a woman on a porch. They stopped and asked her if she knew Pearl. She said yes. Jade said she asked the woman if she knew where our sister and the baby were. The woman said no.

As they walked to the car, the woman came up to them and said in a low voice, "There's a baby in there, and if you want, I will bring him out because I don't think he will last here." She went into the house and brought the child out wrapped in a thin blanket, with only a T-shirt and wet pamper on his tiny body. Jade scolded our nephew for not taking the baby in, took him back home, and proceeded back to her home to care for Marion.

Shocked and horrified at the story, I told her about the dream I had the night before my travel. I dreamt Pearl was walking down the street without a coat, with the baby in one arm and her other arm exposed with needle track marks. She was asking people if they wanted a baby. I was so frightened at what could have happened to this child. The next day, we sat Pearl down and told her that we would help her with her Marion and that she was not alone. Jade said she would be her primary backup, and I stated that I would be number two. I called Lance and told him what happened, and he told me to bring the child home. I told him that was not how things worked. I left Chicago worried about my newborn nephew since he was only a few weeks old.

Several weeks later, I planned to go back to Chicago to check on the situation, but before that could happen, Jade called and said Pearl went to the store to buy Pampers and never returned. She had, in essence, abandoned her child and had been gone for several days. She asked me to come now because she had fallen down the steps and needed help. We called the welfare office in Chicago and informed them of the abandonment and stated Jade wanted to care for the child. They told us to bring our birth certificates to prove our relationship to Pearl. They also told us to file a police report when I arrived in Chicago and bring that to the office as well. When I arrived, we filed a police report, and I brought my birth certificate as instructed. I was not prepared for the next day's drama.

With trepidation, I prepared breakfast, washed, dressed, and fed the baby. I went downstairs to warm the car before going back for the baby and my sister. Struggling on the back porch third floor landing with the baby in a car seat, a diaper bag, and my purse, Jade stopped at the top of the stairs and started shaking. She said that she could not walk down the stairs because she was scared she would fall. I took the baby down the stairs, secured him in a running locked car, and then went back upstairs to assist my sister down the stairs. After finally securing her in the car, checking on the child, who was sweating profusely, and making him comfortable, I drove to the aid office. Since my sister needed help getting out of the car, I had to double park, help her out of the car, escort her into the building, and get back in the car before finding a parking place. I struggled to get the baby, the car seat, diaper bag, and my purse out of the car. I maneuvered around several feet of snow on the curb and walked half a block to the office.

When I arrived, a crowd of people surrounded Jade, as she was crying and shaking, stating that her back was hurting. Immediately, I was pissed! Why was she garnering attention while I was struggling with the baby, a diaper bag, my purse, and a heavy ass coat. I was frustrated to the roof! I settled the child and went over to her and asked her what was going on. She said that her back hurt. I calmly told her to sit down, but she said she could not move. I guided her to a chair, helped her with her belongings, and made sure she was comfortable. I wondered how the hell she got around before I got to town.

Exhausted, I tended to Marion myself. People started glaring at me because they thought I was unnecessarily cruel for not caring for my sister, but I smelled a rat. A short while later, we were called to the back for the interview. The caseworkers asked a series of questions and then requested our birth certificates and the police report claiming child abandonment. I pulled out my birth certificate and the police report and looked to Jade to present her certificate. She searched through her purse and then said that she left her certificate at home. Remarkable! With clenched teeth, I said, "I brought mine all the way from Alabama, and you left yours at home? The whole purpose of this meeting is to prove a relationship," I stated with a stressed tone.

As I was talking to Jade, she started jumping in the chair. A few questions later, while she still had sporadic jerks, the workers left the office. I asked her what the hell was wrong with her, and she told me that she suffered from spasms as a side effect of her injury.

"Well, how long are they supposed to last?" I inquired. "About three months."

"What the hell! How are you going to take care of a child if your recovery is supposed to be three months?"

She said, "I thought you were staying here to help me." Dumbfounded with disbelief, I just put my head down in my hands and said, "What the hell are you talking about? I cannot stay here for three months with you. I have to go home. I have a family and a job."

The workers returned to the office and said, "Here's the problem," talking to Jade, "you didn't bring sufficient evidence relating you to the child's mother, and besides, you don't appear to be in any condition to take care of a child anyway. Therefore, we have decided that the child needs to be put in . . . " I quickly interrupted and said, "He can come and live with me. Tell me what I have to do to take my nephew home." They asked me if I was sure, and I told them, "Yes, tell me what to do." They gave me step-by-step instructions on what was necessary to obtain permission from the courts to take my nephew home. I gathered the baby, my belongings, and told my sister to get her shit, then we left.

The next morning, I headed out the door to start my endeavor in hopes of securing the court's permission to bring my nephew home. The time-consuming task included first obtaining my nephew's birth certificate and then filing paperwork to present my case to the judge. Being that I had never been in a courtroom and was unfamiliar with court proceedings, I was in murky territory. In the registrar's office, I was denied the birth certificate since I was not a parent. In the next building and office, I had the misfortune of speaking with a contentious female who acted like her job was a curse, and I was a hindrance to her day. I was told I was in the wrong office and that my journey was to start six blocks away with a filing, which would direct me back to this office four to six weeks later. Defeated, I turned my back to the counter and cried. I prayed and asked God to please give me the strength to complete my task. I told Him I did not know what to do and asked Him to help me.

After my tears dried, I turned back around and was greeted by three smiling faces, which included the previous woman with the nasty attitude, each asking me if they could help me. I chose to go to the male and told him what I was trying to do. I had to fill out a form showing finances and was told that I did not qualify for assistance though I did not realize I needed financial help. He said that he would circumvent the process and send me upstairs to the judge's courtroom. I left to find an ATM for the court fees, returned, and retrieved the document needed to see a judge.

I took the elevator up several floors, entered the courtroom, went to the front, and told the first desk clerk near the judge what I needed. Offended, she told me that I was not supposed to talk to her, and she pointed me to the next person. The next person told me that I was not using the right words for the courtroom.

I stopped talking, took a deep breath, and said, "Ma'am, I've never been in a courtroom other than to get married. Will you please tell me what words to use?" Once that was settled, she took my paperwork, created a file, and told me to take a seat and wait to be called.

After a couple of hours, the judge called me to the front and asked me why I was there. He then asked me why I didn't just take the baby back to

Alabama, I responded, "Isn't that kidnapping?" He smiled and told the clerk to write up an order for me to obtain the birth certificate. He instructed me to meet with a caseworker because the State of Illinois did not know me and to return to his courtroom after lunch at around three p.m. I walked across the street for the interview.

Once there, I gave my name and within minutes was seated with a worker. Coincidentally, the worker knew my sister and questioned how she was. I explained what was going on, but he did not seem surprised.

Unfortunately, the State of Illinois was very familiar with Pearl, but this worker was somewhat surprised that she had birthed more than a few children since he had last contacted her. I explained her struggles and assured him that her children were in good care. He asked me a battery of questions and concluded by stating he needed to do a background search to find out my status. I left for lunch and returned to the courtroom and waited. The caseworker arrived and moved me to the front of the room, and we both went up when called to speak with the judge. The judge asked me if I had the birth certificate and if I had spoken with the worker. I said, yes. He then asked the worker what he uncovered. The worker responded by stating his preliminary findings resulted in his approval of me taking the child home.

The judge stated, "Well, the State of Illinois does not know her in the courts." The worker responded with, "The State of Alabama does not know her either." With that, the judge gave me permission to take my nephew home with the guarantee of returning in six weeks for a final determination.

We worked out the details, and I left. I went back to Jade's home exhausted, and when she asked me how everything went, I collapsed to the floor and cried. I do not know why I was crying, but I wailed for a good while. She tried to soothe me, but I did not want to be touched. I needed my husband, and I was tired. I went to her room, closed the door, and went to sleep. I believe I was in shock at what I had done. My son was fifteen, and my daughter was in college. I was in school, had a career, and my husband's hard work was finally paying off. I had committed to caring for a baby, a baby I did not know and had to bond with quickly.

Later that evening, I physically became the primary caregiver for my nephew. I immediately thought since his mother had cleaned her system to birth a healthy child, she would come and claim him one day. I decided I would keep the possibility in mind regardless of how much I knew I would learn to love him as my own. News traveled throughout the family that I had taken custody of the baby, but no one offered to back me up. I was disheartened by the lack of offers because Marion's older siblings had called Jade and said they would support her when the plan was for her to care for Marion. No one offering to help me raise Marion was hurtful because I thought this should have been more of a family effort with at least his sisters and brothers offering support. Moving forward, I figured this would be an Alabama thing. Lance and I would raise this child without birthday wishes or the acknowledgment of any other successes, just like it was with our children.

My second eldest nephew, with whom I had an outstanding relationship, called and offered to drive Marion and me back home since I was ill prepared to fly with an infant. I agreed and offered to pay for gas. Once home, we quickly arranged our lives around caring for an infant, which included taking baby pictures in front of the fireplace for his 'later in life' memory book. Through the kindness of coworkers, we were given clothes for a year and a bassinet. I was once again a new mommy, challenged with post-partum depression, sleepless nights, and fatigue.

Experience had taught me how to handle this portion of my life, and all went well. This time around, I had an adult daughter, a son in high school, a niece who had moved down to attend A&M University, some great girl-friends, and Lance.

Four months passed, and I found out Pearl had become pregnant again. I was stunned and left work. Once I got home, I collapsed across my bed and had a good cry. I realized I would raise this child to adulthood. For three days, I was angry, and this affected my child. As I held him, he kept pushing away from me and was so unhappy; his little face looked hurt.

God blessed me with a moment of clarity; I looked him in his eyes and said, "You feel my anger towards your mother, don't you? I am sorry, honey; it is not your fault. I will do better with you than I did with Patricia. I won't put on you any animosity for your mother as I did her." I decided right then that I would do better with this child than I had done with my other three. God blessed me with an opportunity to do better, and I accepted his favor.

After experiencing the joys of his first words, steps, potty training, and birthday, Marion was our son, and he belonged with us. I never thought that

I could love a child I had not given birth to as much as I loved this one, and I realized it was because I had him since he was twelve weeks old. This was my opportunity to raise another woman's child as I had raised my own and be much smarter about it. I vowed to do my best by him and cherish things I did not have the foresight or capacity to instill—as healthy-minded mothers are supposed to do—when the first three were younger. I had a support system, and it made the next few years go by with ease.

We decided to officially adopt Marion and provide him with all the protection and guidance we had given to our other children. My outlook on life had blossomed over the years, and I gained a new respect for my husband. He traveled less, which allowed him to partake in the care of our youngest son. I looked up one day and realized for the first time in my life that I was outnumbered by males. I learned to embrace my newfound protection. I felt safe with so many loving men in my life.

More Challenges

WHILE AT WORK ONE day, a male colleague saw me in the hallway, and we greeted each other in our typical fashion of a handshake. He and I had been working at the same company for more than five years, since I first started working on the same team as the group's admin. On occasion, we spoke in his cubicle or mine, and many times, a large group of us would do lunch. He was a minister and officiated at Alicia's wedding, which meant he was one of the few male coworkers who was invited to our home, as he was not a close friend of mine or Lance.

On this day, after we greeted each other, we passed through a hallway to where there was a conference room with the door open with the lights out. He suddenly grabbed my right arm to pull me in, and I resisted. He pulled my arm harder, and I resisted more and stumbled away from him. Disturbed by his actions, I proceeded to walk to my desk, and he followed me. When I passed the first office on the left, he stepped in and put out his hand. He gestured that he wanted to shake my hand, as if to apologize. He looked strange to me at this point, yet I stepped in to shake his hand, my right to his right.

He then pulled me close to him, looked straight in my eyes, and said in a conniving tone, "You know what I want." Shocked, I stepped back, and as he pulled my hand tighter and me closer to him, he repeated his menacing words while piercing me with his eyes, "You know what I want." I was angry!. I balled my left hand into a fist and hit his right hand as hard as I could. I yanked away from him.

I looked him up and down and said, "Your nerve!" Then I walked to my cubicle. Shaky, disoriented, and angry, I tried to settle down and rationalize what had just happened. For all the years I had known this man, I never expected him to put his hands on me. It was his friend who usually made overt gestures, but I had learned how to talk down his absurd ideas about us dating. The incident made me feel uncomfortable and furious, so when two colleagues came back from lunch, I told them what had happened. They, too, were astonished and questioned what I thought he meant by it. I did not know what he meant; I was confused. I went into the bathroom with the female coworker and took off my long sleeve white shirt. I had bruises on my arm from when he grabbed me. She then believed he touched me and said she did not want anything to do with it.

I went back to my desk and sent him an e-mail expressing my displeasure with his actions and threatened him to not ever touch me again. He responded with an apology without responsibility. Later in the day, I went home bewildered and emotional, as I had started to feel uneasy.

The next day, when I got to work, I felt the need to tell my manager just in case he did it again, but I did not know the protocol. My manager, in turn, reported the incident to HR and I was instructed to report downstairs for an official statement. I replayed my version of what happened and stated I believed in forgiveness and did not want to move forward with a complaint. I was informed it was not my decision, and the matter would be investigated. I went home and had a restless night.

A few days later, I was scared out of my mind. For no discernable reason, I started crying and shaking, fearful for my life. I went back to HR and told them what I was experiencing and was referred to employee resources for free counseling. I had the initial appointment with the therapist, and at the end of the session, she apologized and stated that since the end of the year was approaching, my next appointment would not be until January. I thanked her for her services and went home feeling like she could help me understand why I had suddenly become fearful.

Over the next few days, I became a nervous wreck, dropping glasses, jumping when someone walked up behind me, and, in general, feeling uneasy during the day. A friend at work told me I should press charges with the police department, so I went to the Huntsville office. Once at the counter,

I nervously told the officer what I wanted to do, and he proceeded to take my report.

He stopped writing and said to another officer, "This woman here wants to press charges against a guy because he pulled her arm." Then he looked at me and asked, "You don't like for men to touch you?"

Nervously, I said, "No," and I left. While resting in bed several days later, I felt blood dripping down my face as I relived being shot in the head. It was a surreal moment as I had never experienced anything that had happened in the past in a present state. I walked through the entire ordeal after being shot, from getting up off the floor to standing at the door and pressing the button for the police to come. I felt the blood dripping down the right side of my face, and I knew, at that moment I was vividly reliving a memory. I felt strangely liberated and believed I would be alright.

A few hours later, the phone rang. It was a follow-up call from the police department, questioning me about the report I had filed. He wanted to know what to do with the report and if I wanted to move forward and press charges. I rambled on about how I just wanted something for the record if he did it again because I now understood my fear, then I hung up the phone. But as the days went by, I continued to unravel, and by the time I made it to my next therapy appointment, I broke down to the floor. In the fetal position, I cried until I could cry no more, got up, wiped my face, and asked the doctor what was wrong with me. She told me that when I was pulled into the dark conference room, it triggered memories of being forced into the dark walk-in cooler and shot in the head. She told me I needed to start seeing a therapist who specialized in PTSD. I made an appointment and kept it moving.

I needed to be made whole again, and I knew time waited for no one. Once with the new therapist, I was put on Lexapro, a medication for depression and anxiety disorders. I was advised to take a week off from work to get myself together. Again, I vigorously kept my appointments and learned about triggers. After several weeks, I felt stronger, and life was normal again. My accuser was admonished for his behavior, but I had to learn to work around him.

*****

Sometime after being harassed at work, my brother Lem died suddenly. Being the first death of a sibling, it was very traumatic for me but more traumatic for my sisters living in Chicago. Though the service would be an unfortunate yet pleasant occasion for my family to gather, my sisters' temporary inability to move forward with final arrangements left my brother Clem in Chicago, Terrel in St. Louis, our father in Marvel, Arkansas, and me to pull everything together.

While talking on the phone to Terrel, he asked me why the other girls couldn't handle matters. I answered that they were probably handling stress differently, and if a person doesn't learn how to get over situations, they will remain stuck. I proceeded to tell him how I handled stressful situations in my life and that I didn't think our sisters addressed their stress or problems in a healthy manner. He went on to ask me how I dealt with stress and I provided the wrong example. I accidentally told him about being sexually harassed at work. I immediately tried to retract my statement, but Terrel didn't fall for it when I tried to change the topic.

He asked, "What's this guy's name?" Again, attempting to change the topic, I went back to the death of our brother. He said, "And where does he live?" I changed the topic again. He said, "Why won't you answer my questions?" Calmly, I stated that I did not want any violence. Notoriously, he stated, "I'm not gonna hurt him for real. I just want to get some of my boys to come down there, take him out to the field and snatch on him a li'l bit." I did not give up his name.

We traveled to Chicago for the solemn event and thankfully, the gathering from beginning to end was without drama. It was pleasant as it was one of the rare occasions where we were all together with our parents.

*****

Another episode of anxiety was dealt when an employee at a facility in Meridian, Mississippi, unloaded his shotgun on several coworkers. He was angered because he was forced to attend ethics and diversity training due to the many complaints filed against him.

When I heard about the shooting, I said, "This is not supposed to happen here." As I watched the massacre unfold on the television in the lobby, I repeated to someone, "This is not supposed to happen here."

He said, "No, it's not."

I waited for my work buddies, and we all went to lunch. A conversation about the shooting ensued, as it was a white man killing black coworkers. I repeated, "This is not supposed to happen here."

Once back at work, I felt uneasy and panicky. I went to my functional manager's office and said, "You know, John, that shooting today wasn't supposed to happen here."

He looked at me and said, "No, Val, it is not." I stood shaking and unhinged in his doorway. He looked at me and said, "Go home." I turned around and proceeded to walk to my desk. I heard a girlfriend call my name, but I ignored her and walked faster.

She sped up and touched my shoulder and said, "Girl, didn't you hear me call you?"

I screamed, "Don't touch me!" and ran down the hall. She came after me, and I ran to the wall and started crying, "They're gonna shoot me; they're gonna shoot me!"

I begged her to take me home. She walked me to my desk to get my purse and told me to wait so that she could get hers. Crying and trembling, I put on my sunglasses as she guided me out the building to her car and took me home. I called the daycare and told them my girlfriend would come and pick up my son. She kept him until I woke up and asked her to bring him home.

Later in the day, I called my counselor who specialized in PTSD, and made an appointment. Once seated with him, we discussed my new problem and set a goal to learn how to separate fiction from reality. I went back on Lexapro as I had stopped taking it after the last incident. We agreed I would need about eight weeks of therapy. I returned to work after a week's absence and performed my tasks as expected.

Heightened awareness for workplace violence had become unreal as I did not see how I could change careers again. My vigor for normalcy became an integral priority and learning to deal with stress was paramount for survival. Fortunately, during my counseling sessions, I left no stone unturned, as we discussed all the problematic matters in my life. After a few short weeks, I improved, and my counselor told me I had what doctors in his field called 'mental toughness,' which gave me the ability to heal quicker than others when mentally and emotionally challenged.

Indeed, over time, I relied on this as truth, but I also learned there were some things in life over which I had no control, and it was best to learn to fight through adversity instead of succumbing to defeat. Several occasions triggered my anxiety, such as a local college shooting, where an aggrieved employee took the lives of her colleagues at the campus. The shooting happened right across the street from where I worked. The sight of the police cars and realizing I was headed in the same direction after work put me in a panic. I rushed home and poured wine into a 32oz cup. I drank it while stuffing a row of thin mint cookies in my mouth. I was glued to the television set, watching the event unfold. I went to work the next day, shaken yet not as fragile.

Then there was the massacre at the theatre in Colorado where a young, adult male unleashed hell on the patrons during the Batman Returns movie. I loved the Batman series but had to wait until it was released on cable before I could enjoy it; however, I was pleased with myself when I was able to go to the theatre and watch a different movie.

Lastly, the Sandy Hook Elementary School massacre froze me with fear. I refused to watch anything pertaining to the event because I knew those visuals would push me over the edge since I knew I would not have been able to find any way to deal with this level of violence. Though I knew the nation had to deal with these mass shootings, and the parents' loss was unimaginable, for me, learning no one was coming to shoot me down was important for my daily reality.

*****

As time moved on and my family thrived, I continued with my education with hopes of completing my degree. However, Marion had been diagnosed with Attention Deficit Hypertension Disorder (ADHD) when he was in kindergarten. He required more of my patience than any child had in the past, which made me stop and go with my schooling. Lance and I learned that everything we had done in the way of communicating and punishing our older children was akin to giving this child a one hundred dollar bill.

The doctor gave us tools to start implementing behavior modification methods since, by this time, Marion was learning his way. I used the egg timer to reward good behavior throughout the day, and it was working until he found the basket of wrapped gifts and decided to take them all. I also worked more closely with his teachers on ways to keep him focused and encouraged while at school. He basically stayed in trouble throughout his elementary school days, but by the time he was in the seventh grade, his behavior started to improve. Before starting the eighth grade, he asked to be taken off his meds because he no longer got in trouble while at school. He stated he did not like the way he felt and decided to control himself.

When Marion was eight years old, we heard his older brother, Cris, who lived with my brother Terrel and his family, was not happy. All had been going well in my brother's home until Terrel went on an extended business trip out of the country, and due to his absence, Cris started acting out. Lance said we should bring him here to raise the boys together. The summer of Cris' twelfth birthday, we went to St. Louis and brought him to live with us.

Once we got home from St. Louis, our first task in bringing the boys together was to have them share a room so that they could bond. While they knew each other, as we would always get Cris if he was in Chicago while we were visiting, or on our short visits to St. Louis, they never spent more than a few days together. Now, it was important for them to learn to live as brothers.

Bringing home another child with emotional needs interfered with my schooling, so I stopped again. The first few months were difficult, but after the first year, it all seemed to fit together. At least, that is what we thought until Marion wrote a letter expressing his strong dislike for his brother. Because he was being bullied, he asked that we send him back. Saddened by this letter, I asked Cris to write a letter expressing how he felt about his new home to get each side of the story. Once completed, I had the boys read their letters out loud, and Marion did so with ease. On the other hand, Cris did not want to, so I read his. My eyes teared up reading his words because he immediately took responsibility for mistreating his little brother and said that is how he had always been treated and did not know any other way. He thought that is what brothers were supposed to do because their two older brothers had done the same to him.

Remembering the pain from my childhood caused me to take a break from them to compose myself. I then shared my family history with them and told them how damaging it was to my sisters and me to be taught how to mistreat one another and how it carried over into our adult lives with our own children. I told them we had to do better as a family because when all was said and done, we had to depend on and trust one another in our immediate family before expecting anything from anyone else. I also told them God brought us together for a reason, and we must never ask why, yet be grateful for His blessing.

From that day on, the boys worked on their relationship, and things got better and normal, but they were still kids, and they fought and scrapped the way kids do. When Cris started high school, we separated the boys into their own rooms so he could have some independence, and the older would not overtly expose his little brother to too much teenage life. Each boy thrived in school and played sports. After rec football, they played school ball. The most important thing going on in my life at that point was providing for these two young men and witnessing Lance take on the full responsibility of mentoring and caring for their emotional well-being as a father. I came to realize how lucky I was as a woman to be falling in love with my husband again. Our blessings started to double, and my appreciation for my family heightened. I felt stronger and more encouraged to finish my education.

*****

By the time Cris came to live with us, Lance Jr. was in college at the University of Alabama at Tuscaloosa. He had graduated from high school with honors, and after accepting a full football scholarship with Stillman College in Tuscaloosa, the next year he transferred to the University of Alabama. He took advantage of this opportunity and as a walk-on made the football team. We were exceptionally proud of him. His ability to make the team came with a tinge of overconfidence and a smirk at life, or so it seemed.

The mindset of some athletes is nurtured by privileges allowed by schools and, at times, creates impudence in young men. Our mission was to instill in him responsibility for his actions and have him complete his college degree, which he did. Alicia had married a man named Earl, whom I love as my son, became a mommy, graduated from college, and enjoyed her life as a fitness instructor. Patricia still lived in Los Angeles and had become a single parent. She had built a life for herself on the West Coast, and we made sure she visited for major events such as graduations and her sister's wedding. Lance and I had started over with Cris and Marion and did our best to provide for them, so they too had the same opportunities as our older children to be college-educated and prosperous individuals.

Sadly, Patricia still struggled with her place in the family. While living in Los Angeles, she escaped a major health issue and needed to regroup. I offered her solace in our home since I thought we were finally strong as a unit and could provide comfort to her and her son. Lance had become the man and head of our household I needed him to be, and I had his unyielding support in family matters.

After several months of living in our home, tensions between Patricia and I caused many disruptions. This time around, Lance backed me up when we argued. I felt stronger with my husband's support; therefore, nothing stopped me from completing my degree. I took care of my home, had date nights with Lance, and studied in the evenings. We grew closer as a family with firm support for one another. Unquestionably, my husband is one to behold and cherish. My love for him exponentially grew as I witnessed his dedication to Cris and Marion. Parenting the boys allowed Lance to see how difficult it was for me to mother his daughter.

Lance and I had started working harder to achieve success, which enabled us to start over with our nephews. We never complained or looked for anyone to help us out with their needs, as we were in the position to care for them. We had come to learn the phrase *"To whom much is given, much is expected."* We gave freely from our hearts to all our children with zero regrets. I fell in love with my husband all over again, and we began to enjoy our lives as two people who had survived the disagreements, outside parents, dysfunction with our children, and the strain and stress of any long-standing marriage. I finally had help in rearing children and no longer felt alone.

Change is Nothing New, but Damn!

One day, I wrote down all my work duties and started training people to cover for me while on short-term leave due to back surgery. I felt as though I was replacing myself. Within a few weeks of returning to work, I was told my services were no longer needed in the form of a R.I.F., Reduction in Force. The program I was working on was entering the maintenance phase, and all work was reduced by fifty percent. I was given a ninety-day notice, which was more than enough time to find more work.

One of my previous managers needed my expertise on another contract, and I accepted. As time went by, I interviewed and was awarded another position, pending contract award. I separated from my place of employment after fourteen and a half years in September 2011, and in essence, I left my family.

During my employment, I had given the company my all, as I volunteered for all employee groups and helped shaped the attitudes in the facility. After I turned in my badge, I cried all the way home. In my mind, I played a slow-motion video, starting from the first day I interviewed as a secretary and my promotion to a database administrator, to my transition to a senior software configuration manager.

I started back at school, again online, one last time to complete my degree and obtain certificates in my field in preparation for my new position. Unfortunately, my company did not win the contract and I was officially unemployed. I tried and was unable to secure work. In fact, it would be three and a half years before I went back into the workforce. Until then, I continued the coursework for my degree, supported the boys at basketball games and other school events, and dated my husband. We were grandparents, and over time, all of our children were living close to our family home. Again, things seemed to be going well.

I talked with my daddy on Sundays and we maintained a beautiful relationship. He went with us when we took Lance Jr. to Stillman College, which warmed my heart. He was proud of his grandson and that made me happy since he was absent during my school years. Two years later, on November 24, 2005, Lance Jr.'s twentieth birthday, my daddy died. The loss of my father encouraged me to work things out with my Mother. We worked to reconcile most of our differences. I would call her at least twice a week, just to hear her voice. I had come to respect my mother on a parenting level; I struggled to raise five children and she had fourteen.

After twelve years, I completed my Bachelor of Science Degree in Management and was re-established in corporate America. But another struggle was yet to come.

*****

Every year on the anniversary of being shot in the head, I sought a different reason to appreciate the blessing of life. In the early years, the appreciation was simply life itself. I would say "God, thank you for allowing me a chance to do better." Over time, the gratitude was for personal successes, such as overcoming difficult situations and fighting through anxiety. As my children aged, it was being thankful for raising them without seeing them turn into negative statistics, i.e., not graduating from high school, not going to college, not becoming teen parents, or standing in front of a judge for breaking the law and going to prison. Some years I had to dig deep to find a celebratory reason but I always found something.

However, thirty-three years to the day of being shot in the head on April 17, 2017, my husband had a stroke. Life was moving along, and Lance had retired from work while simultaneously caring for his father in our home. His dad had come to live with us in August 2016, the weekend after we took Cris to college. Lance had gone to Chicago to assess the dire need for his parents to be cared for with his other siblings. He called and told me no one's household could care for them both and his father desperately needed care. I immediately stated he could come live with us. I changed Cris' room to Lance's father's room and felt proud. I though it remarkable how quickly I was able to adapt to change but after I video chatted the room for Lance to see, I became numb. When the call ended, I quickly walked to my bedroom and closed the door. Once inside, I rushed to the bathroom, closed that door, and went into the walk-in closet. Once secure and in a private space, I screamed and howled my pain. I realized I was exhausted and needed a break. I was tired of helping other people and wanted out. I felt helpless.

Lance came home a few days later. Everything seemed to change instantly with a stranger in the house. His father had only visited us once, in our first year of moving to Alabama. To be honest, his presence was something to get used to. However, and as usual, we adjusted to the new family structure. Lance did his best to care for a man who had been primarily absent in his life. Though his parents had been married for more than sixty-two years, he failed to be present during our thirty-two-year marriage. Nevertheless, his dad needed assistance, and Lance gladly stepped up. He cared for his father, and I cared for my husband.

With many years of experience supporting family members in our home, we took on this new challenge with the same vigor and determination. However, this time around, we were presented with more of a challenge. My problem was that my husband never retired and he was being pulled and stretched beyond his emotional capacity. Men do not think the way women do, and like most men, Lance was a fixer. As time passed, I convinced Lance to go back to playing racquetball and finding some time for himself. Lance's schedule gave our children opportunities to spend one-on-one time with their grandfather. Once a week, Lance met with friends for lunch and went to the gym. Finally, some normalcy for Lance. While he was establishing boundaries with his dad, he finally scheduled his long-needed partial knee replacement surgery. The impending surgery had become the optimal time for a caregiver to come in and assist with his dad. I rallied for continued long-term assistance, and I had hoped this would be the start of Lance's retirement.

Then, on April 17, 2017, thirty-three years to the day from when I was shot, Lance began having troubles. I was getting ready for work, when Lance said,

"I can't move my arm."

"Well, can you move your leg?" I asked.

He said, "No."

I instantly thought, *He's having a stroke*, and walked over to the bed. I saw him floundering, trying to sit up, and I stood to balance him in case he fell. When he finally sat up, he fell backwards. I cupped his face with my hands, and as I looked into his eyes, I said, "Baby, what's wrong?"

He laid back on the bed with exasperation and said, "I'm having a stroke."

I laid my left hand on his chest, reached across him, and dialed 911. While talking to the operator, I picked up my cell phone, called Marion, and told him to come into the room; we had an emergency. I was given instructions on what to do for Lance, and I gave our son instructions on preparing and opening the door for the paramedics. Remarkably, Lance was talking to the operator and the emergency crew when they arrived. I asked him to stop talking and try to relax because we were both talking at the same time; however, I stepped out of the way and let them communicate with the patient. I watched in dismay as they carried my husband to the roll-away bed and out of the house. He told me not to cry because he could not handle that. I had to suck it up and be strong for him.

Marion drove me to the hospital, and I methodically went down the list and called our children, his brother Arthur, and my sister Jade to help get the word out. It appeared to me at that moment, nothing was real, and this was all a dream. I struggled with what I had done wrong to cause this burden to my husband. Was I too mean to his dad? Was I insensitive to what he was going through? Did God feel the need to test me again to prove my devotion to my husband? Over the next few days, I stated, "I did not see this one coming." When asked who could have seen it or what that meant, I stated, "I thought we were good, and we had done enough over the years, and the rest would be easy." I eventually said, "We plan, but God is the best planner."

Lance suffered from an Ischemic stroke caused by a clot formed in his brain, which cut off the blood supply to the vessels. Unfortunately, Lance was not a candidate for a reversal medicine called t-PA (tissue plasminogen activator) because one of the major side effects was a brain hemorrhage, and since he had an AVM, the chances were too high. The t-PA could have dissolved the clot and minimalized the damage of a stroke. The only other recourse was to increase his blood pressure to increase newly oxygenated blood into his brain and start with rehabilitation therapy. Realizing the last option was the only choice, Lance and I chose this road for recovery.

Later in the day, Lance was admitted into the NICU, and our journey began. He sadly told me all he wanted to do was retire and go fishing. He cried and when I left the hospital, I cried again. From then on, my actions towards Lance were nothing but positive, and I was willing to do whatever was necessary to restore his health. He suffered paralysis on his right side. Having had my personal struggles and demons, I could not imagine how it felt to no longer take care of yourself. My heart was heavy for my husband, and I was scared about what would happen next. As the children and I waited, and Arthur came down to handle matters for their father, I set on a path to make our home peaceful and harmonious. It was agreed his father would have to relocate to an assisted living home. With Lance and Arthur's permission, I set out to find a facility.

After a week's absence from work, I returned to my daily duties and visited my husband every day when I got off work. Now in the rehabilitation unit, each day, Lance showed me something different. He started improving immediately once his therapy started. I cried when he sat up on the side of the bed for the first time a week later. He went from floundering with frustration on a Monday to sitting up with little ease eight days later. My pride in him swelled in my heart as I witnessed a little progress each day. Eagerly and with soft, loving eyes, Lance showed me what he could do without introduction, as he realized I was looking at his every move.

Gauging every nuance of his being, I silently watched him as I tried to determine how I could help make anything easier for him. Monday through Saturday, Lance had physical and occupational therapy, and each day when I came to visit, I saw him flourish. He told me after he cried the first night, he decided he would make the best of his time and work on being better and stronger. Our routine had become for me to call when I got off work, then we decided what to eat for dinner. I stopped by stores to get little things to make his day comfortable and purchased food. We sat in his room, ate dinner, and watched television. I pushed him in his wheelchair down the hall, and we chatted about the day. I brought his father to visit only once, as it was a challenge getting him to and from the facility. Once home, I made sure my father-in-law had dinner, checked in on our son and made sure his needs were met, then settled for the evening. Since Cris had started college the weekend before Lance's father moved in, I did not have to worry about his daily needs. I was exhausted and frustrated, but what held me together was simple; my husband had it worse. My local girlfriends stayed in touch but eventually stepped back and gave us private time. My brother-in-law came to town again to settle legal matters for their father, and we moved his father to an assisted living home two weeks before Lance's homecoming. Twenty-six days after his stroke, Lance came home. This was an entirely new struggle, and I worried about what could go wrong, yet each day, little by little, the sun peeped in the sky, and I found a sense of joy.

Conclusion

Our oldest daughter Patricia and her son moved from our home to their own. She started back to school and completed her degree. She is employed as a top-level manager for an insurance company where her promotions keep her busy. My first-born Alicia and her husband Earl graduated from A&M, and her family prospered while her husband went from being a private to a civilian employee. She is a full-time mom and works in her ministry. After our oldest son Lance Jr. graduated from college, he put his efforts into playing professional football, making it to the semi-pros. He spent time in Sweden as the Offensive Coordinator for the Uppsala 86ers and training kids to play American football. Our middle son Cris graduated from junior college with a technical degree in welding and is working in his field. Our youngest son Marion is at home and is taking a gap year from college; he is our 'test baby' because he got the best of us. His parents are smarter, seasoned, tried, and proven to be good at what they do. He is happy and low-key with just enough vigor to make me smile. When his brothers were away, I told him he must hug me for each of his brothers, and he just smiled and said okay.

Learning humility and allowing people to help me was synonymous with strength as I struggled with each. My strong faith in God's will gave me breath; however, trust in mankind was my personal demon. People have disappointed me so much in my life; therefore, I always struggled to let more than a small few in and witness my pain. Lance and I continue to work together on our journey to be whomever God has created us to be. He is my guy, and I am his girl. We see the light at the end of the tunnel, and we are walking into the light together.

A little girl from the projects of Chicago who lived in rough neighborhoods, overcame physical, mental, and emotional abuse, endured struggle, strife, homelessness, and single parenting, a survivor of violence who had been shot in the head, overcame the odds of failure, completed her degree, and had secured an opportunity to become part of corporate America. I had indeed found a pearl in a sea of oysters destined for me alone and I would make the best of it and take this journey as far as I could without fear of failure or flight.

The End

CPSIA information can be obtained
at www.ICGtesting.com
Printed in the USA
LVHW011915091021
700009LV00015B/616